THE ONE YEAR®

Adventure with

THE GOD OF YOUR STORY

BRIAN HARDIN

NavPress

A NavPress resource published in alliance
with Tyndale House Publishers, Inc.

NavPress is the publishing ministry of The Navigators, an international Christian organization and leader in personal spiritual development. NavPress is committed to helping people grow spiritually and enjoy lives of meaning and hope through personal and group resources that are biblically rooted, culturally relevant, and highly practical.

For more information, visit www.NavPress.com.

The Team:
Don Pape, Publisher
Caitlyn Carlson, Acquisitions Editor
Elizabeth Schroll, Copy Editor
Jennifer Ghionzoli, Designer

Cover and interior illustration of art deco patterns copyright © Cartur Argi/TRNTFF/Creative Market. All rights reserved.
Designed by Jennifer Ghionzoli.

For information about special discounts for bulk purchases, please contact Tyndale House Publishers at csresponse@tyndale.com, or call 1-800-323-9400.

Cataloging-in-Publication Data is available.

ISBN 978-1-63146-837-7

Printed in China

25 24 23 22 21 20 19
7   6   5   4   3   2   1

CONTENTS

introduction

DECEMBER 31 · *day 0*

WELL, HERE WE are. Together at the beginning. You may be feeling daunted by the idea of reading through the entire Bible over the course of this next year. And the Bible is an ancient, oversized book, to be sure. That's the problem most of us face when approaching it. We struggle to know how (or where) to begin. Part of that is because the Bible isn't one singular book, but rather a collection of sixty-six different writings, originally inspired in Hebrew, Aramaic, and Greek over millennia. Those different writings contain historical narrative, poetry, apocalyptic literature, wisdom tradition, public and private letters, prophecy, and Gospel narratives. Of course it's confusing! The Bible is a massive corpus that spans thousands of years of time and covers thousands of miles of geography.

But the Bible is a lot more approachable than we might think. You see, the Bible captures and preserves the account of God's unwillingness to be left out of the human story—and when we realize that, we soon discover that God is also unwilling to be left out of our own story. Understanding this changes everything, because the stories found in Scripture mirror our own lives profoundly.

If we approach the journey ahead as a relationship rather than a chance encounter or as a symphony rather than a pop song, we will quickly settle into a rhythm that will carry us from the first verse of Genesis to the final phrase of Revelation. And believe me, you will find much treasure between those two points as the God of your story reveals Himself.

Using these daily readings in conjunction with your own daily reading from *The One Year Bible*, you will be able to enjoy and appreciate the entire Bible without getting lost—and perhaps for the first time, the Bible will speak to you on its own behalf. Each day, we'll conclude with something to further think about or a moment of worship or prayer.

Obviously, we'll encounter all the famous stories we learned growing up. We'll also pass through all the famous passages that we quote to one another continually—but we'll experience them in their native context and understand why they were written in the first place, which is surprisingly important to how we understand their power in our lives. Even if we're students of the Bible who have spent much time and energy attempting to distill theological understandings, we still must remember to slow down and allow God's Word to unpack us, rather than the other way around.

If we'll settle into this rhythm, over the next year, the Bible will begin to have its own voice—and it will be the voice of a friend who is always honest. Many days, we will wonder how we ever negotiated life without this daily honesty in our lives.

This is the journey we are about to embark on. Our voyage will take 365 days and will be the journey of a lifetime. It's much easier to dream about than to do,

I admit. But this can be your year. You really can do this. All you have to do is show up every day. The Bible you might have been avoiding is about to become the best friend you've ever had.

Having said all that, a final word of counsel before we begin: Look in the mirror. Look at yourself inwardly and consider how your life feels right now. Perhaps you are anxious about the future. Maybe, for the first time, you feel lost within your own being. Perhaps the past year has brought you bloodied and limping to the Bible as a final hope. It doesn't matter. You are here now. Right now matters. Everything that comes next matters. Take a mental snapshot and remember this moment and how it feels. Three hundred and sixty-five days from now, you will look in the mirror and see a different person—if you show up every day.

This book comes from fourteen years of showing up every day, seven days a week, and allowing the Bible to speak as I've given it voice on the Daily Audio Bible.* It also comes from two hard years of distilling what has come from that spoken work into written form. I have done my best to show up and offer a pathway through the Bible that will allow irreversible change from within. The rest is in your hands. The choices you make over the next 365 days will determine the story of your year. Make the Bible a daily decision. The journey awaits.

---

* For ease of understanding, I sometimes interject the speaker's name when quoting Bible passages in daily readings.

JANUARY 1 · *day 1*

Genesis 1:1–2:25; Matthew 1:1–2:12; Psalm 1:1-6; Proverbs 1:1-6

OUR JOURNEY BEGINS as all must—at the start, or in the beginning. Today's reading is an important first step, because knowing where we've come from gives us the context we need to properly observe our own life's story.

"In the beginning God created the heavens and the earth" (Genesis 1:1). These words launch us into the grand adventure. In one year, we will travel many dusty miles and meet deeply fascinating people who will become meaningful friends—for they are our spiritual ancestors. In their stories, our own hearts will be revealed.

Since we're at the beginning, let's orient ourselves to the territory we will first encounter in the Old Testament. Genesis is part of a larger grouping of writings that encompass the first five books of the Bible (Genesis, Exodus, Leviticus, Numbers, and Deuteronomy). This grouping is called the Torah, or the Pentateuch. When we consider the book of Genesis, normally we think about the Creation story. But Genesis covers more time than any other book of the Bible—more time than the remainder of the Old Testament combined. Within the first eleven chapters of Genesis, we will cover a couple of millennia and a couple of thousand miles before slowing things down and focusing on several specific generations of people who fundamentally shape the rest of the Bible and influence our world today.

On this first of 365 days, we see God's care and intentionality with all His creation. Our human experience has been fashioned in God's own image, deriving its animating life source from the breath of God Himself. According to the Scriptures, we exist not by chance but by intention. Each of us is supposed to be here, and we each bear the image of a God who is intertwined with our story much deeper than cells and atoms.

Today we get an amazing and rare view of how things were always supposed to be for us: a perfect world with perfect people created in God's image. When we contrast this image of perfection with the world we currently live in, we get a sobering sense of how the story has turned over the millennia—but we'll get to that over the next few days.

Together, we'll be surprised by how often what we read in the Bible will mirror our own hearts and motives. And we'll be delighted to understand that God is not a distant and uninterested Being. He is deeply invested in the human story and deeply in love with what He has fashioned.

Oh, the joys of those who do not follow the advice of the wicked, or stand around with sinners, or join in with mockers. But they delight in the law of the LORD, meditating on it day and night. They are like trees planted along the riverbank, bearing fruit each season. Their leaves never wither, and they prosper in all they do.   PSALM 1:1-3

JANUARY 2 · *day 2*

Genesis 3:1–4:26; Matthew 2:13–3:6; Psalm 2:1-12; Proverbs 1:7-9

TODAY'S READING UNVEILS one of the saddest stories in the Bible. We know this story as "the fall of man," and it reveals the trajectory of the rest of Scripture. This story is the beginning of the larger story: the reason for God's willingness to come here in the person of Jesus to rescue His creation.

In the Garden of Eden, God offered Adam and Eve the tree of life and prohibited them from the tree of the knowledge of good and evil. It's easy to wonder at the purpose of a prohibited fruit. But this tree gives us an incredible picture of how deeply invested God is in a first-person relationship with us. True love isn't something that can be faked. Enslavement can shape someone's behavior—if the consequences are dire enough—but authentic and true love can only be offered freely from the heart. Love can't be true if there is no way out. And the tree of the knowledge of good and evil appears to be exactly that.

Unfortunately, a deception was hatched, and our first mother and father dreamed of becoming like God, tragically forgetting that they already were. Adam and Eve chose to eat, contrary to God's command, with devastating repercussions. The catastrophic depths of this choice is revealed in God's heartbreaking question: "What have you done?" (Genesis 3:13).

"I was naked, so I hid,"[1] was the response. We have been hiding ever since. We see it every day in the way we interact with each other. We curate and present our best selves while hiding who we really are. The trade was perfection and true love in exchange for knowledge, and we have attempted to use that knowledge to imitate Sovereignty—with frightening and terrible results.

Throughout history, humankind has worked to remain self-directed, but this has not brought us back to God. We will not find our way back to God. Only God can bring us back to Himself, and He is. This is the story of the Bible.

MEDITATION:
Serve the LORD with reverent fear, and rejoice with trembling.   PSALM 2:11

---

[1] Author's paraphrase.

JANUARY 3 · *day 3*

Genesis 5:1–7:24; Matthew 3:7–4:11; Psalm 3:1-8; Proverbs 1:10-19

IN OUR FIRST few days, we've gained a context for the stories that are beginning to unfold before us. Yesterday, we learned of humankind's fall from perfection and complete intimacy with God. Murder and death entered the human story—things we were never intended to endure.

Today in Genesis, we jumped a millennium into the future and saw the devastating results. Humankind had become so corrupt that they acted as animals and had only evil intentions. God regretted creating them. To see us so far from our created state of perfection and intimacy grieved His heart (Genesis 6:5-6). But there was one righteous man: Noah. And we saw a redemptive thread weaving its way into the story as a reset of the earth came by way of a great flood.

Since we took a moment a couple of days ago to orient ourselves to the book of Genesis, we should also consider the first book of the New Testament, and the first of a grouping of four books known as the Gospels: Matthew.

When Matthew became a disciple of Jesus, he left his prosperous former life altogether. He had to. He had previously been a tax collector and was considered a betrayer of his people, the Jews.

Although Matthew appears first in the New Testament, it is likely the second Gospel chronologically, with Mark being first (we'll get to that later). Matthew was written in Greek but was originally intended for a Jewish audience. We know this because it quotes from the Hebrew Scriptures (Old Testament) more than any other Gospel and reveals Jesus as the Hebrew Messiah by demonstrating the ways in which Jesus fulfilled Hebrew messianic prophecies.

In today's New Testament reading, we followed Jesus as He went into the wilderness, where Satan challenged Him. While in the wilderness, the evil one tempted Jesus with an invitation to abort his mission and inherit the earth the easy way. All Jesus needed to do was bow to him. Jesus was the first perfect person to walk on the earth since Adam, and Satan put the same type of humanity-twisting temptation before him. But Jesus made a different choice: He rebuked the evil one and sent him away.

We confront similar temptations every day. And we either respond to them like Adam and Eve—or like Jesus. Each of us daily choose whether to eat of forbidden fruit or to know God by intimately walking with Him in every thought, word, and deed. How will you choose today?

WORSHIP:
You, O LORD, are a shield around me; you are my glory, the one who holds my head high. PSALM 3:3

JANUARY 4 · *day 4*

Genesis 8:1–10:32; Matthew 4:12-25; Psalm 4:1-8; Proverbs 1:20-23

TODAY IN GENESIS, we watched the floodwaters recede and Noah and his family once again place their feet on dry ground. Scripture unfurls a list of the generations that followed, revealing the ways in which the earth's population grew and spread.

In Matthew, we saw Jesus' earthly ministry begin and how He called together men who left everything behind to follow Him. We'll get to know them well, for they become the band of brothers who will walk alongside Jesus throughout His ministry.

Our reading from Psalms today hits us between the eyes, but before we get to that, let's begin to understand what we are reading when we read from the psalms. Believe it or not, Psalms is actually five books in one, and we'll notice when we're moving into another book because it's announced. The books are largely separated by author, theme, or purpose, and from antiquity, the Psalms have been considered a priceless collection of 150 of the most beautiful songs, hymns, congregational singings, individual songs, and poems of worship the world has ever seen.

A voice we will truly get to know in the Psalms will be that of Israel's second king, David. Although we will be offered an intimate portrait of this courageous and deeply human king in 1 and 2 Samuel and 1 Chronicles, the Psalms will reveal his heart.

"Don't sin by letting anger control you. Think about it overnight and remain silent," the poet-king David told us in the Psalms today (4:4). David will teach us a lot about ourselves in the days ahead. After all, how often are we reactionary, as if life is happening to us rather than the other way around? David gave us compelling advice that echoes across the millennia. Imagine the immediate effect it would have on our daily lives if each of us was not controlled by anger and allowed for silence and perspective instead.

"Come and listen to my counsel. I'll share my heart with you and make you wise," we read in Proverbs, as if to bring the point home (Proverbs 1:23). May we accept this invitation and make space in our lives for wisdom to guide us.

MEDITATION:
You can be sure of this: The LORD set apart the godly for himself. The LORD will answer when I call to him. PSALM 4:3

JANUARY 5 · *day 5*

Genesis 11:1–13:4; Matthew 5:1-26; Psalm 5:1-12; Proverbs 1:24-28

IN OUR READING from Genesis, humankind planned to build a tower to the heavens as a memorial to themselves. But again, God intervened. We were never intended to be sovereign unto ourselves. Self-sufficiency is contrary to our true nature, which is to be intimately connected with God. So God disrupted the plans at Babel—He confused the language of the people, and humans spread across the earth as a result.

In Matthew's Gospel, Jesus began to teach one of His foundational messages, known as the Sermon on the Mount. This disruptive message describes a world that we long for but have no idea how to achieve—which may be the point. Like the people at the tower of Babel, we cannot achieve the life we long for by our own cunning and ingenuity. We may accomplish marvelous things, but without a total dependence on God, we are completely unable to fill the void within ourselves. Jesus spoke of the countless blessings for those who reach the end of their own strength and ability, only to find God there. We are happiest when we depend on God for everything we are and everything we ever will be.

May we truly depend on God today in every choice we make and word we speak, knowing that we are safe in His care when we live in the light and walk in truth. It's our choice.

In Proverbs today, we see that this choice has always been before us:

I called you so often, but you wouldn't come. I reached out to you, but you paid no attention. You ignored my advice and rejected the correction I offered. Proverbs 1:24-25

These words resonate because we know we've been that person. But this is a new day. May we pay vigilant attention to the voice of Wisdom as we move forward. We'll be surprised at how often it will snap us awake and clearly speak clarity into immediate situations.

PRAYER:
Let all who take refuge in you rejoice; let them sing joyful praises forever. Spread your protection over them, that all who love your name may be filled with joy.   PSALM 5:11

JANUARY 6 · *day 6*

Genesis 13:5–15:21; Matthew 5:27-48; Psalm 6:1-10; Proverbs 1:29-33

YESTERDAY, WE GOT a brief introduction to a man named Abram, who we'll get to know much better in the coming days. Eventually, his name will become Abraham, and the reverberations of his life echo until today—for it is through him that the faith we freely enjoy finds an anchor.

God called Abram to a land he did not know and promised him that the land—as far as he could see in all directions—would one day belong to his family. This land would eventually become known as the "Promised Land." There was a problem, though: Abram was getting old and had no children to inherit the land, regardless of the promise. God invited him outside and, against the backdrop of an immense sky of stars, told him:

5

Look up into the sky and count the stars if you can. That's how many descendants you will have! Genesis 15:5

Abram had faith in God at that moment, and God considered him righteous because of it (Genesis 15:6). Abraham's faith is going to become very, very important when we begin to explore Christian doctrine through the eyes of the apostle Paul.

The next time you have a moment of uncertainty regarding your faith, go outside and look at the stars. Remember that God is faithful to those who trust Him.

In the Proverbs today, the voice of Wisdom shows us the alternative to trusting God:

They hated knowledge and chose not to fear the LORD. They rejected my advice and paid no attention when I corrected them. Therefore, they must eat the bitter fruit of living their own way, choking on their own schemes. Proverbs 1:29-31

We have a choice in this. We can fall into the overwhelming grace of a loving God by doing nothing more than trusting and intimately walking with Him, or we can choke on our own schemes. This is always the choice before us, but it's not because God is pompous or tyrannical. It's because this is how we were made—to know and be known by God.

PRAYER:
Return, O LORD, and rescue me. Save me because of your unfailing love.
PSALM 6:4

JANUARY 7 · *day 7*

Genesis 16:1–18:15; Matthew 6:1-24; Psalm 7:1-17; Proverbs 2:1-5

ABRAHAM RECEIVED A promise from God that his progeny would one day inherit a Promised Land. But Abraham had no children. And in today's reading, God told Abraham how He was going to fulfill His promise.

"I will return to you about this time next year, and your wife, Sarah, will have a son!" God told Abraham (Genesis 18:10).

Sarah overheard this and laughed to herself because she was too old to have children. But God confronted her and reiterated that she would in fact bear a son.

What have you been holding out hope for in life? What if you were promised, "About this time next year . . ."? Would hope rise? Or have you been laughing at the impossible?

In our New Testament reading, Jesus has much to teach us about living in the Kingdom of God. Throughout His life on earth, Jesus was the picture of true servanthood, and His words point us to how we should live:

If you're going to help somebody, don't make a big deal about it, broadcasting your good deeds so that you get praise and affirmation. If that's what you're after, then you already have your reward. But if you want to find a correct heart's posture, don't even let your left hand know what your right hand is doing. Do it in secret, and your Father, who sees in secret, will give you your reward.

When you pray, don't be fake and proclaim elaborate and complex prayers so everyone can see how "godly" and "spiritual" you are. Go into your private room, pray to your Father in secret, and he will hear you.[2]

And then—a statement that we ignore at our own peril: "If you forgive those who sin against you, your heavenly Father will forgive you. But if you refuse to forgive others, your Father will not forgive your sins" (Matthew 6:14-15).

Mic drop. Jaw drop.

Forgiveness is not an option in God's Kingdom. But forgiveness does not mean that we pretend things didn't happen. Rather, it means that we have a place to release those people and events in our lives that may have sabotaged us for too long. Forgiveness is a command—yes—but it's also an invitation to the emancipation of our souls. When we forgive, we are forgiven.

WORSHIP:
I will thank the LORD because he is just; I will sing praise to the name of the LORD Most High.   PSALM 7:17

JANUARY 8 · *day 8*

Genesis 18:16–19:38; Matthew 6:25–7:14; Psalm 8:1-9; Proverbs 2:6-15

IN OUR OLD Testament reading today, we witnessed the destruction of Sodom and Gomorrah. God came and verified for Himself the evil reputation of the civilizations in the Jordan valley, and He did not let their sin stand.

But as devastating as the scene is, we find amazing beauty in how God engages with Abraham here. Abraham's nephew Lot was among those living in the valley, and God first asked, "Should I hide my plan from Abraham?" (Genesis 18:17). Was this a rhetorical question? Why would God ask if He didn't want to share His heart? And why would He want to share His heart if He didn't want Abraham to know it?

A conversation ensued in which Abraham asked God if He would spare the towns if fifty righteous people were present. Then forty-five. Then forty. Then thirty. Then twenty. Then ten. What's beautiful about this exchange is that God was willing to have the conversation. As Abraham continued to negotiate lower numbers, God's response revealed the truth: God wasn't interested in indiscriminately causing destruction. The presence of the righteous could certainly hold

---

[2] Author's paraphrase of Matthew 6:1-5.

off the judgment people were bringing on themselves. But sadly, not even ten righteous people were there.

Meanwhile, Jesus spoke intimately about our daily lives. His words in today's reading alone offer us another penetrating look in the mirror and an example of what it looks like to be one who follows Jesus.

Jesus instructed us clearly not to worry about what we'll eat or what we'll wear. "Can all your worries add a single moment to your life?" He asked (Matthew 6:27). "Don't worry about tomorrow. . . . Today's trouble is enough for today" (Matthew 6:34).

As encouraging as these words are, though, Jesus' teachings became more sobering: "Do not judge others, and you will not be judged. For you will be treated as you treat others. The standard you use in judging is the standard by which you will be judged" (Matthew 7:1-2). In other words, all those reactionary assumptions and opinions we form about others is the standard by which our lives will be measured.

In the end, Jesus tied all that He was saying into an attitude we must cultivate and live into if we want to find a life of wholeness, become Christlike, and know God:

> *Seek the Kingdom of God above all else, and live righteously, and he will give you everything you need. . . . Do to others whatever you would like them to do to you. This is the essence of all that is taught in the law and the prophets. You can enter God's Kingdom only through the narrow gate. . . . The gateway to life is very narrow and the road is difficult, and only a few ever find it.* Matthew 6:33; 7:12-14

Knowing and following God is a choice—a difficult one, because it requires utter vigilance and awareness of what is going on around us, and all our heart, mind, and strength. But nevertheless, the choice is ours. May we be one of the few who find the narrow path that leads to life.

MEDITATION:
What are mere mortals that you should think about them, human beings that you should care for them? Yet you made them only a little lower than God and crowned them with glory and honor. PSALM 8:4-5

JANUARY 9 • *day 9*

Genesis 20:1–22:24; Matthew 7:15-29; Psalm 9:1-12; Proverbs 2:16-22

TODAY WE READ of the fulfilment of a promise: a son named Isaac, born to Abraham and Sarah. Abraham had two sons, Ishmael and Isaac. Ishmael was born because Sarah gave her servant Hagar to Abraham as a surrogate. As disturbing as this arrangement might seem to us now, it was a common practice of the day. But Sarah's choice displayed her lack of trust in God's promise, and the decision resulted in relational problems. Sarah demanded that Hagar and her son be sent away after the birth of Isaac, but God rescued and provided for them.

Soon, it appeared as if Abraham would also lose Isaac, for God asked Abraham to travel to Moriah and sacrifice Isaac to Him. This is certainly an unsettling story, but it begins to reveal not only the covenant that Abraham and God shared but also Abraham's unflinching trust in and devotion to God—for which he became a patriarch of the faith. In a covenant, nothing can be withheld. And because Abraham was in a covenant with God, he would not withhold the gift of Isaac, even though he was a promised child. In the end, God provided the offering. He never intended to have Isaac sacrificed.

"Because you have obeyed me and have not withheld even your son, your only son," God said, "I swear by my own name that I will certainly bless you. I will multiply your descendants beyond number, like the stars in the sky and the sand on the seashore. Your descendants will conquer the cities of their enemies. And through your descendants all the nations of the earth will be blessed—all because you have obeyed me" (Genesis 22:16-18).

We can easily see the tension in the story. Putting ourselves in this position seems impossible. And yet, much later, God stepped into the place of the Father sacrificing his Son. He loved us so much that He would not withhold His only Son to save His people. This is how much we are loved.

WORSHIP:
I will praise you, LORD, with all my heart; I will tell of all the marvelous things you have done.   PSALM 9:1-2

JANUARY 10 • *day 10*

Genesis 23:1–24:51; Matthew 8:1-17; Psalm 9:13-20; Proverbs 3:1-6

ALTHOUGH WE'RE ONLY a week and a half into the adventure through the Bible this year, we've covered significant ground. We've moved through more than a millennium in time and a thousand miles together—but before we move forward, let's recap briefly. In Genesis, we've discovered our origin story, which gave us context for how things in the world got the way they are. We've journeyed through the story of Adam and Eve and humanity's spiral downward, which resulted in a great flood. We've read the story of Noah. We've also met Abraham, whose family touches everything else that happens in most of the Bible.

Today, the second generation after Abraham took center stage as Isaac's mother, Sarah, departed in death. Abraham secured a family burial field and cave called Machpelah, among the Hittites in the city of Hebron. The city still exists today, as does the burial cave; it's one of the holiest places in the world for Muslims, Jews, and Christians alike.

Abraham had become a very old man with little time left on his human journey. But before he died, he wanted to ensure that Isaac had a suitable spouse, not only to carry forward the family tree but also to protect the promise. The dramatic search back into Abraham's former homeland introduced us to the lovely Rebekah.

In the New Testament, a ranking Roman officer—a man acquainted with and accustomed to power—came to Jesus, pleading for healing for his servant. He didn't order (or even ask) Jesus to leave what He was doing to travel to heal the servant. "Lord, I am not worthy to have you come into my home," he said. "Just say the word from where you are, and my servant will be healed. I know this because I am under the authority of my superior officers, and I have authority over my soldiers. I only need to say, 'Go,' and they go, or 'Come,' and they come. And if I say to my slaves, 'Do this,' they do it" (Matthew 8:8-9). Jesus was astonished at the officer's faith, and the bedridden servant was healed.

In both our Old and New Testament readings today, the counsel of the book of Proverbs was lived out in living color:

> *Trust in the LORD with all your heart; do not depend on your own under-standing. Seek his will in all you do, and he will show you which path to take.* Proverbs 3:5-6

With these examples, we are given a road map for our own lives. From this proverb, we receive a succinct encapsulation of the underlying wisdom. This will often be the case with Proverbs because it is the centerpiece of the Wisdom Literature of the Bible. Wisdom Literature speaks in a direct but poetic manner, as opposed to narrative style, in which a story is told and meaning is gleaned. Wisdom Literature speaks volumes in sentences.

To truly appreciate the sayings in Proverbs for what they are, we must under-stand that these are the collected wisdom of the ages distilled and disseminated largely by Israel's third king (who is renowned to this day for his wisdom), Solomon.

Using surprisingly few words, these proverbs have the power to cut through the clutter and shake us awake. If we'll pay attention to the proverbs each day, take hold of them, and guard them as the key to life (Proverbs 4:13), they will rescue us when we're about to step into foolishness and lead us wisely in every decision we make.

MEDITATION:
The LORD is known for his justice. The wicked are trapped by their own deeds. PSALM 9:16

JANUARY 11 · *day 11*

Genesis 24:52–26:16; Matthew 8:18-34; Psalm 10:1-15; Proverbs 3:7-8

IN OUR READING from Genesis today, after 175 years of life on earth, Abraham died. The God of Abraham became the God of Isaac. Meanwhile, Isaac and Rebekah married and had twin sons of their own—Jacob and Esau.

"The sons in your womb will become two nations," God told Rebekah. "From the very beginning, the two nations will be rivals. One nation will be stronger than the other; and your older son will serve your younger son" (Genesis 25:23). We will watch this dramatic struggle unfold in the coming days.

In Matthew, Jesus calmed a Galilean storm as His terrified disciples watched in speechless astonishment. "Why are you afraid?" He asked them. "You have so little faith!" (Matthew 8:26).

If we're paying attention, we'll begin to see the theme of faith everywhere in both Old and New Testaments. It's either spoken or demonstrated in the lives of the people we meet in the Bible. Faith is the glue in these stories and is no less a requirement to know God and live a life within His presence today.

We have a much easier time masking our lack of faith when it is within our power to act out of our own strength. But within the torrent of a storm like the one Jesus calmed, the truth is always revealed. We either panic and blame God for something He had nothing to do with or reach in faith toward God. It might seem as if this call to dependence is unkind on God's part, but God is fathering us in this process. We would be profoundly unloving and unkind if we did not guide and parent our own children into maturity, and those of us who are parents understand the challenges involved in protecting, nurturing, and disciplining our children. For our children to thrive, they must have faith in our love and protection. The next time we go kicking and screaming to God because things have moved beyond our control, let's remember the kicking and screaming of our toddlers and calm down. Perhaps we are simply being presented with an opportunity to grow up. God loves us and wants us to become mature sons and daughters of His Kingdom. But maturity is impossible to attain without faith—and the Bible will continue to show us this as the larger story of redemption continues to progress.

MEDITATION:
The wicked arrogantly hunt down the poor. Let them be caught in the evil they plan for others.   PSALM 10:2

JANUARY 12 · day 12

Genesis 26:17–27:46; Matthew 9:1-17; Psalm 10:16-18; Proverbs 3:9-10

ISAAC WAS AGING and losing his eyesight. The first generation after Abraham was rapidly moving toward the grandchildren's generation, and the tension foretold by God between Jacob and Esau was on full display. In today's Old Testament reading, we saw a generous amount of trickery between the brothers. Esau had previously sold Jacob his birthright for a bowl of stew, but in today's reading, Rebekah and Jacob conspired to get Isaac's final blessing before his death—and they succeeded.

But all was not well and good for Jacob after this. He had to go on the run from Esau's rage, fleeing back toward his ancestral homeland. In the process, he missed the later years of his father's life, the love of his mother, and the comfort of his home.

Meanwhile, in Matthew's Gospel, Jesus had confrontations of His own to deal with. "Be encouraged, my child! Your sins are forgiven," Jesus told a paralyzed man who had been brought before Him in hopes of healing (Matthew 9:2). This proclamation of forgiveness set off the teachers of religious law. They accused Jesus of one of the most grievous offenses possible: blasphemy. Despite this, He healed the man right in front of them, saying, "Is it easier to say 'Your sins are forgiven,' or 'Stand up and walk'?" (Matthew 9:5). This kind of behavior would eventually turn the religious establishment against Jesus and would become the grounds for sentencing Him to death. But Jesus didn't have a lot of tolerance for hypocrisy, as we see in the many confrontations He had of this nature.

Jesus always entered a person's story. He was more than willing to buck the system to get to a person's heart. After the healing of the paralyzed man, He met a man named Matthew (whose Gospel we are currently reading). The people of Israel detested Matthew because he was a tax collector, and yet Jesus ended up at his house, along with other tax collectors and sinners.

"Why does your teacher eat with such scum?" the Pharisees asked Jesus' disciples (Matthew 9:11).

If we're honest, we find that we've held similar attitudes. The Pharisees prided themselves on avoiding interactions with sinners and people of ill repute—and sometimes, so do we. But Jesus never did. He always found the plot behind the story in a person's life. Jesus said:

> *"Healthy people don't need a doctor—sick people do." Then he added, "Now go and learn the meaning of this Scripture: 'I want you to show mercy, not offer sacrifices.' For I have come to call not those who think they are righteous, but those who know they are sinners."* Matthew 9:12-13

Had the Pharisees paid attention to Jesus' words, they would have discovered that they weren't as healthy as their outward appearance indicated. But before we judge them, we must first examine our own lives—because we may be no better off. Too often, we, too, present a false image. Let's consider the ways in which we are the Pharisees in this story. Considering ourselves rightly will lead us toward fundamental and necessary changes. After all, our pursuit is to be like Jesus, and we will never grow in that direction if we spend our energy judging others and pretending to be something we're not.

MEDITATION:
Honor the LORD with your wealth and with the best part of everything you produce. Then he will fill your barns with grain, and your vats will overflow with good wine. PROVERBS 3:9-10

JANUARY 13 · *day 13*

Genesis 28:1–29:35; Matthew 9:18-38; Psalm 11:1-7; Proverbs 3:11-12

AS JACOB FLED to the north and away from his brother, Esau, he stopped at the city of Luz to sleep. Here the God of Abraham and Isaac revealed Himself to Jacob in a vision of a stairway to heaven, reaffirming His promise that one day He would give the land to the family of Abraham.

"Surely the LORD is in this place, and I wasn't even aware of it!" Jacob said when he awoke (Genesis 28:16). Jacob renamed the place Bethel, which means, "house of God" (Genesis 28:19). Its ruins remain today, and the terraced terrain indeed looks like a stairway.

Jacob made a vow at Bethel:

If God will indeed be with me and protect me on this journey, and if he will provide me with food and clothing, and if I return safely to my father's home, then the LORD will certainly be my God. *Genesis 28:20-21*

And thus, the God of Abraham and Isaac became the God of Jacob.

In Matthew's Gospel, Jesus stepped into a funeral that was a bit premature. A synagogue official's little daughter was gravely ill, and the desperate father sought Jesus out. But the girl died before they could return. A crowd of people had assembled, and the funeral dirges were already underway.

Jesus chased everyone off. "The girl isn't dead; she's only asleep," He said (Matthew 9:24). And these words turned their mourning into laughter, but not in a good way. The people mocked Jesus because they'd seen the girl, and as far as they were concerned, she was dead. But Jesus approached her and lovingly reached for her hand. She stood up, to the obvious amazement of the onlookers.

Our reading today invites us to ponder many of the impossible situations in our lives. Would our mourning turn to mocking laughter if we heard the words "It's not dead; it's only asleep"? Or would we, like Jacob, declare, "Surely the LORD is in this place, and I wasn't even aware of it"?

MEDITATION:
The LORD corrects those he loves, just as a father corrects a child in whom he delights.   PROVERBS 3:12

JANUARY 14 · *day 14*

Genesis 30:1–31:16; Matthew 10:1-23; Psalm 12:1-8; Proverbs 3:13-15

IN OUR READING from Genesis yesterday and today, Jacob arrived in his ancestral homeland and was welcomed by his uncle Laban. He fell in love with Laban's daughter Rachel and offered to work seven years to marry her, but the morning after the wedding brought quite a surprise—Rachel's older sister, Leah, was lying next to him. He'd slept with the wrong girl! Laban made Jacob work another seven years for Rachel, his true love.

In the end, the sisters Leah and Rachel were married to the same man, and only one of them was loved. This favoritism caused conflict and initiated a war between the sisters to provide the most children. But these children are extremely important to the biblical narrative, as we shall soon see.

As deliberately cunning as Laban was toward Jacob, God used Jacob's time in Laban's household to eventually make Jacob very wealthy. But Jacob longed to return to the land of his father, Isaac—which would be no small task. Jacob and his wives made a plan and left secretly while Laban was away.

Today in Matthew's Gospel, Jesus sent His disciples out for some on-the-job training, effectively giving them instructions for what to do after He was gone. Essentially, He said: "Go. It doesn't have to be far away; there's no need for fanfare or publicity. You don't need anything to do it but your presence. Go to the adrift, perplexed people around you. Tell them that the Kingdom is near. You've been treated generously, so live generously." Jesus gave us this same permission and instruction to go out into our neighborhoods—into our spheres of influence—and tell people about the incredible offer of salvation. And Jesus' words complement today's reading from Proverbs, which says that having wisdom—operating in life with clarity and direction—is worth far more than money or power or anything else we could desire.

Know and walk with God today, and live with purpose. Hear the words of Jesus, and *go*.

MEDITATION:
Wisdom is more profitable than silver, and her wages are better than gold. Wisdom is more precious than rubies; nothing you desire can compare with her.   PROVERBS 3:14-15

JANUARY 15 · *day 15*

Genesis 31:17–32:12; Matthew 10:24–11:6; Psalm 13:1-6; Proverbs 3:16-18

IN OUR GENESIS reading today, we witnessed an anxious time for Jacob. He, his wives, their children, and the entire household fled Laban, and Laban gathered his men and pursued them. Despite plenty of drama in the following events, the two men eventually formed a tense treaty and parted on good terms.

Once he'd dealt with the concern behind him, Jacob had to immediately turn to the apprehension in front of him: his brother, Esau. Although a couple of decades had passed, the brothers had not parted on good terms. Jacob had shrewdly purchased Esau's birthright and stolen his father's blessing. The relationship between them, as it had been left, was unhealthy, to say the least.

Jacob sent messengers ahead of the caravan to try to get clarity on what he was about to run into. When the messengers returned, the news was not good. Esau was on his way to meet them with four hundred of his men.

We've all encountered situations like this—when we've been overwhelmed by anxiety, stumbling over a new problem as soon as we've solved an existing one. Our reading in Psalms shows us that King David felt this way as well: "O LORD, how long will you forget me? Forever? How long will you look the other way?" (Psalm 13:1).

The times that test our faith have purpose: They are a barometer for our souls. Who do we really believe in? In whom are we actually placing our trust? We must imitate the posture and prayer of Jacob as he faced the prospect of losing everything:

> *"O LORD, you told me, 'Return to your own land and to your relatives.' And you promised me, 'I will treat you kindly.' I am not worthy of all the unfailing love and faithfulness you have shown to me, your servant. . . . O LORD, please rescue me from the hand of my brother, Esau. . . . But you promised me, 'I will surely treat you kindly, and I will multiply your descendants until they become as numerous as the sands along the seashore—too many to count.'"* Genesis 32:9-12

WORSHIP:
I trust in your unfailing love. I will rejoice because you have rescued me. I will sing to the LORD because he is good to me.   PSALM 13:5-6

JANUARY 16 · *day 16*

Genesis 32:13–34:31; Matthew 11:7-30; Psalm 14:1-7; Proverbs 3:19-20

JACOB'S FEAR OF his brother, Esau, was front and center today in Genesis. Jacob obeyed God by returning to the land of his birth, but the circumstances were dire. Knowing that Esau and four hundred men were on their way to meet him was daunting. Jacob divided his camp so that if they were attacked, perhaps some could escape.

That night, Jacob wrestled with an unnamed man until daybreak. "Let me go, for the dawn is breaking!" the man shouted at Jacob, to which Jacob replied, "I will not let you go unless you bless me" (Genesis 32:26).

Jacob received a blessing, but he also received a name change. And this change snaps many of the pieces of the Old Testament thus far into place, clarifying where the road ahead is leading us.

"'Your name will no longer be Jacob,' the man told him. 'From now on you will be called Israel, because you have fought with God and with men and have won'" (Genesis 32:28).

To this point, Jacob had been blessed with eleven sons, given to him by his two wives and their maidservants. He would eventually have a twelfth son. Before this night, those sons were known as the sons of Jacob. But after the name change, we immediately realize that these are Israel's sons—the *children of Israel*! And the lineage from each of these sons will become the twelve tribes of Israel. But we'll have to wait for that story. There are many miles we must travel beforehand.

Today in Matthew's Gospel, Jesus told us,

Come to me, all of you who are weary and carry heavy burdens, and I will give you rest. Take my yoke upon you. Let me teach you, because I am humble and gentle at heart, and you will find rest for your souls. For my yoke is easy to bear, and the burden I give you is light. Matthew 11:28-30

Like Jacob (Israel), we all face times when we do not understand the road in front of us. We also go through seasons when it feels as if we're wrestling with God. In these times, our heart's posture is a true measure of our faith. Jesus offered us an extraordinary invitation: We don't have to navigate our lives to avoid anxiety and hardship. Yes, both will visit each of us from time to time. But we can find rest in Jesus. This means that if we can follow Jesus' example of humility and gentleness of heart, then we will be walking the pathway that leads to rest for our souls.

MEDITATION:
The LORD looks down from heaven on the entire human race; he looks to see if anyone is truly wise, if anyone seeks God. PSALM 14:2

JANUARY 17 · *day 17*

Genesis 35:1–36:43; Matthew 12:1-21; Psalm 15:1-5; Proverbs 3:21-26

AFTER JACOB AND Esau were reunited as brothers, Jacob moved within the land that had been promised to him. Jacob and Esau were both so prosperous that one region was too small for them both. As we moved along with Jacob and his family through Genesis today, we also said good-bye. Jacob's beloved wife, Rachel, died in childbirth. The child was the twelfth son of Jacob (Israel), and he was named Benjamin (Genesis 35:18). And so today, we read the first recap of the first children of Israel—the names of the sons of Jacob.

Knowing these names and where they came from is important. In the future, these men's names will become the tribes of Israel, and we will cross paths with them frequently as we move forward through the Scriptures.

But we have one more good-bye. Jacob's father, Isaac, died in today's reading as well, at the ripe old age of 180. Jacob and Esau buried him together. Abraham's grandchildren and great-grandchildren now lead the way forward.

In our Psalms reading today, we received answers to questions we've probably asked ourselves (and God) at times: *How do I make this faith journey work? What does a person who is doing it right look like?* Or as King David put it, "Who may worship in your sanctuary, LORD? Who may enter your presence on your holy hill?" (Psalm 15:1).

Thankfully, the Scriptures answer this question:

Those who lead blameless lives and do what is right, speaking the truth from sincere hearts. Those who refuse to gossip or harm their neighbors or speak evil of their friends. Those who despise flagrant sinners, and honor the faithful followers of the LORD, and keep their promises even when it hurts.

Those who lend money without charging interest, and who cannot be bribed to lie about the innocent. Such people will stand firm forever. Psalm 15:2-5

MEDITATION:
Don't lose sight of common sense and discernment. Hang on to them, for they will refresh your soul. They are like jewels on a necklace.
PROVERBS 3:21-22

JANUARY 18 · *day 18*

Genesis 37:1–38:30; Matthew 12:22-45; Psalm 16:1-11; Proverbs 3:27-32

JOSEPH WAS ONE of the two sons of Rachel, Jacob's beloved wife. Today, we saw Joseph's story begin to take shape, and we'll be chasing his story in the coming days. Joseph plays a pivotal role in the promise of God to Abraham, Isaac, and Jacob, but—as we often discover in our own lives—his route was not laid out in a straight line.

Because Rachel was Jacob's favored wife, Joseph was his favored son—and his brothers were jealous. Somehow, the jealousy was tolerable . . . until Joseph started having dreams. His dreams seemed to indicate that one day, his brothers would all bow down to him. We can only imagine the new levels of tension this brought to the family.

One day, Jacob sent Joseph to check on his brothers, who were shepherding their flocks far to the north. When they saw him coming, they decided to kill him. Thankfully, they did not carry out that plan. However, they did something nearly as unspeakable—they trafficked their own brother into slavery. Joseph ended up a long way from home: in Egypt, where he was purchased by Potiphar, who happened to be Pharaoh's captain of the guard.

We all walk through seasons that do not seem fair. Perhaps we've endured a heartbreaking betrayal or another kind of injustice. In these times, our faith is tested—and we should look at testing for what it is. In science, something is tested to find out its composition or to discern if it is pure. Testing is not a bad thing. It gives us answers. And in the case of faith, testing shows us what we are really made of.

Often, in times of testing, we misinterpret what is happening and find ourselves wandering into bitterness. As the story of Joseph unfolds, we will find ourselves staring into our own soul. Joseph was a young man who had every right to be bitter. What happened (and will happen) to him was certainly unjust and unfair. But let's watch his responses at every turn, for they will inform and instruct our own.

PRAYER:
Keep me safe, O God, for I have come to you for refuge. I said to the LORD, "You are my Master! Every good thing I have comes from you." . . . LORD, you alone are my inheritance, my cup of blessing. You guard all that is mine. . . . I know the LORD is always with me. I will not be shaken, for he is right beside me. No wonder my heart is glad, and I rejoice. My body rests in safety. PSALM 16:1-2, 5, 8-9

JANUARY 19 · *day 19*

Genesis 39:1–41:16; Matthew 12:46–13:23; Psalm 17:1-15; Proverbs 3:33-35

WE PICKED UP the story of Joseph today in Genesis. Joseph had been trafficked into slavery by his brothers, who faked his death. His father, Jacob, deeply grieved the loss of his favored son. Meanwhile, Joseph quickly found favor with Potiphar in Egypt. In a short time, Joseph ran Potiphar's entire household. It could have been a decent life—if not for Potiphar's wife. Joseph was a young, attractive, and well-built man, and Potiphar's wife lusted for him. Over and over, she attempted to get him into bed, but he would not betray Potiphar. Eventually, he had to flee the woman, leaving behind his cloak. Scorned, Potiphar's wife used the cloak as evidence against Joseph, landing him in an Egyptian prison.

Joseph had done nothing wrong, but things went from bad to worse. If anyone had a right to claim injustice and become bitter, it would have been Joseph. But God was with him. In short order, Joseph was in charge of the prison.

Joseph began interpreting dreams while in prison—and he was accurate. He rightly foretold the execution of one of Pharaoh's officials while predicting the restoration of another. But still, two years passed, and Joseph remained hidden and forgotten. He had plenty of time to give up hope and sink into bitterness and depression—but he didn't.

When Pharaoh had a dream that his magicians could not interpret, the restored official remembered Joseph. But we'll have to wait until tomorrow to see what happens next.

As the story continues to unfold, we begin to see that there was more going on than Joseph could have known. The circumstances he was living in were dismal. His freedom had been stolen. He was thrown into prison, despite being faithful and loyal. He was forgotten in a faraway land and thought dead by his father. But somehow, Joseph never lost sight of his faith in God.

PRAYER:

O Lord, hear my plea for justice. . . . You have scrutinized me and found nothing wrong. I am determined not to sin in what I say. I have followed your commands. . . . My steps have stayed on your path; I have not wavered from following you. I am praying to you because I know you will answer, O God. . . . Show me your unfailing love in wonderful ways. By your mighty power you rescue those who seek refuge from their enemies.   PSALM 17:1, 3-7

JANUARY 20 · *day 20*

Genesis 41:17–42:17; Matthew 13:24-46; Psalm 18:1-15; Proverbs 4:1-6

"IT IS BEYOND my power to do this," Joseph told Pharaoh after being asked to interpret Pharaoh's disturbing dreams. "But God can tell you what it means and set you at ease" (Genesis 41:16).

Joseph must have been experiencing a bit of culture shock. He grew up in the land of Canaan until he was sold into slavery by his brothers. His slave life was short because false accusations landed him in a dungeon for years. To then be hauled from prison, given a proper bath and shave, and whisked in front of the Pharaoh of Egypt must have been disconcerting. A wrong answer could have ended his life or sent him back into the dungeon.

Despite all that Joseph had gone through, he did not waver from his source of devotion, and God gave him the interpretation to Pharaoh's dreams. "The next seven years," Joseph told Pharaoh, "will be a period of great prosperity throughout the land of Egypt. But afterward there will be seven years of famine so great that all the prosperity will be forgotten in Egypt" (Genesis 41:29-30).

Joseph offered strategic suggestions for how Pharaoh could prepare for this future. Pharaoh quickly appointed Joseph to implement his plan. And just like that, Joseph went from a dungeon to being second-in-command over the land of Egypt.

Seven years later, after Joseph had prepared Egypt for hard times, the famine hit. It was so widespread that it affected Joseph's homeland, and before long, Joseph's brothers were in Egypt, bowing before him as he had dreamed they would so long ago. But they didn't know who he was—which is a story for another day.

Although there are many twists and turns before us in Joseph's story, it's important that we begin seeing the long view. Everything that happened to Joseph up to this point was utterly unjust. Overwhelming sorrow and consuming bitterness would be totally understandable in circumstances like these. But that's not the story. Somehow, Joseph didn't lose faith and didn't blame God. He believed that he was part of a larger story—and that his current circumstances were not the final chapter.

When we find ourselves in a long season where our faith feels as if it has bottomed out, we must remember the long view. There is more going on than we can see, and our Father is good.

PRAYER:
I love you, LORD; you are my strength. The LORD is my rock, my fortress, and my savior. . . . He is my shield, the power that saves me, and my place of safety.   PSALM 18:1-2

JANUARY 21 · *day 21*

Genesis 42:18–43:34; Matthew 13:47–14:12 Psalm 18:16-36; Proverbs 4:7-10

IN OUR READING from Genesis today, Joseph accused his brothers—who still did not recognize him—of spying. They vehemently denied the accusation, and Joseph told them,

If you really are honest men, choose one of your brothers to remain in prison. The rest of you may go home with grain for your starving families. But you

must bring your youngest brother back to me. This will prove that you are telling the truth, and you will not die.   Genesis 42:19-20

As they stood in front of Joseph, the brothers began to lament what they'd done so long ago. They believed that what was happening was God's judgment. They didn't know who he was and that he could understand what they were saying. Their repentance brought him to tears, but he hid his emotions and sent them away.

Once the brothers returned to their homeland, they told their father, Jacob, that they could get no more provisions from Egypt unless they took Benjamin back with them. Jacob flatly refused. He'd already lost Joseph, and Benjamin was the only remaining son of his beloved wife, Rachel. But when the food ran out again, he had no choice.

When the brothers returned to Egypt, they went to Joseph's house to meet with him. Joseph hadn't seen his younger brother since he was a child. "May God be gracious to you, my son," he said and then rushed from the room and wept intensely in private (Genesis 43:29).

Despite his distress, Joseph wasn't yet ready to reveal himself. After all, other than Benjamin, these were the very people who had trafficked him. He needed to know their hearts. We saw this kind of wisdom described today in Proverbs:

Getting wisdom is the wisest thing you can do! And whatever else you do, develop good judgment. If you prize wisdom, she will make you great. Embrace her, and she will honor you.   Proverbs 4:7-8

Following in Joseph's footsteps requires us to slow down and be observant. Let's practice wisdom today.

MEDITATION:
[The LORD] reached down from heaven and rescued me; he drew me out of deep waters. He rescued me from my powerful enemies. . . . He led me to a place of safety; he rescued me because he delights in me.   PSALM 18:16-17, 19

JANUARY 22 · *day 22*

Genesis 44:1–45:28; Matthew 14:13-36; Psalm 18:37-50; Proverbs 4:11-13

TODAY IN GENESIS, we reached the great revelation—Joseph told his brothers who he was. After hiding items once again in the brothers' grain sacks, Joseph forced them to confess at the risk of Benjamin's freedom.

Amid the tension, Judah stepped forward:

"My lord, I guaranteed to my father that I would take care of the boy. I told him, 'If I don't bring him back to you, I will bear the blame forever.'
"So please, my lord, let me stay here as a slave instead of the boy, and let the boy return with his brothers. For how can I return to my father if the boy is not with me?"   Genesis 44:32-34

In this confession, Joseph discerned his brothers' hearts. The men who had once tried to destroy him now were willing to sacrifice themselves for Rachel's other son. Joseph couldn't hold his secret inside any longer. After sending all his assistants and servants from the room, Joseph revealed his identity through tears, to the stunned silence of his brothers.

Don't be upset, and don't be angry with yourselves for selling me to this place. It was God who sent me here ahead of you to preserve your lives. . . . God has sent me ahead of you to keep you and your families alive and to preserve many survivors. So it was God who sent me here, not you!
Genesis 45:5, 7-8

That, friends, is the long view in this story. Joseph had legitimate reasons to sink into despair and bitterness. The ordeal he endured was unjust and had cost him many of his formative and vital years, yet he never lost sight of God's presence, and he never blamed God for his circumstances. He knew that there must be more going on than he could see. And in this knowledge, he stayed true. He trusted God and could see His hand in the entire process. Joseph's trust is a fantastic example of Romans 8:28: "We know that God causes everything to work together for the good of those who love God and are called according to his purpose for them."

We must believe this and take the long view. It is essential for how we interpret the different seasons of our lives.

WORSHIP:
The LORD lives! Praise to my Rock! May the God of my salvation be exalted! PSALM 18:46

JANUARY 23 · day 23

Genesis 46:1–47:31; Matthew 15:1-28; Psalm 19:1-14; Proverbs 4:14-19

ALL THE PIECES of Joseph's story came together in today's reading from Genesis. The brothers returned to their father, Jacob, with the miraculous news that his beloved son Joseph was still alive and had become second-in-command of Egypt, subordinate only to the Pharaoh. As Jacob and his family began the long journey to Egypt, God came to Jacob, reiterating the promise He'd given before: "I am God, the God of your father. . . . Do not be afraid to go down to Egypt, for there I will make your family into a great nation" (Genesis 46:3).

Once they arrived in Egypt, Jacob was reunited with his son. It was as if Joseph had returned from the dead. Father and son embraced each other through tears of joy until Jacob spoke: "Now I am ready to die, since I have seen your face again and know you are still alive" (Genesis 46:30).

This is how the children of Israel came to the land of Egypt. It would be another four centuries before they would depart.

As we moved forward in Matthew's Gospel, Jesus clarified the way life works:

It's not what goes into your mouth that defiles you; you are defiled by the words that come out of your mouth. . . . For from the heart come evil thoughts, murder, adultery, all sexual immorality, theft, lying, and slander. These are what defile you. Eating with unwashed hands will never defile you. Matthew 15:11, 19-20

Life is not outside in. We live from the inside outward. We can spend our entire lives trying to surround ourselves with comfort and luxury, but neither of those things will fill the void within. Only in understanding that life flows from within us—from our hearts—can we begin to cultivate life as it was intended. Our hearts must belong to God. When we know and walk with God intimately, the source of life itself is within us and spills over into our exterior world.

PRAYER:
May the words of my mouth and the meditation of my heart be pleasing to you, O LORD, my rock and my redeemer. PSALM 19:14

JANUARY 24 · *day 24*

Genesis 48:1–49:33; Matthew 15:29–16:12; Psalm 20:1-9; Proverbs 4:20-27

IN OUR GENESIS reading today, we said good-bye to Jacob. He was 130 years old at the time of his reunion with Joseph. He died at 147, but not before blessing Joseph's sons, Ephraim and Manasseh, and then pronouncing his final blessing over all his sons.

"Soon I will die and join my ancestors," Jacob then told them. "Bury me with my father and grandfather in the cave in the field of Ephron the Hittite. This is the cave in the field of Machpelah, near Mamre in Canaan, that Abraham bought from Ephron the Hittite as a permanent burial site. There Abraham and his wife Sarah are buried. There Isaac and his wife, Rebekah, are buried. And there I buried Leah. It is the plot of land and the cave that my grandfather Abraham bought from the Hittites" (Genesis 49:29-32).

This wish was carried out—in royal fashion. A grand procession returned to the land of Canaan and buried Jacob in the cave of Machpelah in the valley of Eshcol. Let's remember this location. We encountered it first with Abraham (which was centuries ago), and we'll be visiting it again centuries from now with great consequence.

In today's reading from Proverbs, we received a megadose of essential and absolute truth: "Guard your heart above all else, for it determines the course of your life" (Proverbs 4:23).

Our hearts are where we commune with God, and our intimacy with God indeed charts the course for our lives. Giving our hearts to unworthy things can become like drinking from a tainted water source that is corrupt and will make us sick. Our hearts are ground zero for our lives, and we must be intentional, vigilant, and wholly devoted if we want to know and be known by God.

BENEDICTION:
In times of trouble, may the LORD answer your cry. May the name of the God of Jacob keep you safe from all harm. . . . May he grant your heart's desires and make all your plans succeed. . . . May the LORD answer all your prayers.   PSALM 20:1, 4-5

JANUARY 25 · *day 25*

Genesis 50:1—Exodus 2:10; Matthew 16:13–17:9; Psalm 21:1-13; Proverbs 5:1-6

TODAY WE CONCLUDED the first book of the Bible with a farewell to someone we know well—Joseph. At 110 years of age, Joseph spoke his final words to his brothers:

Soon I will die . . . but God will surely come to help you and lead you out of this land of Egypt. He will bring you back to the land he solemnly promised to give to Abraham, to Isaac, and to Jacob.
. . . When God comes to help you and lead you back, you must take my bones with you.   Genesis 50:24-25

The second book of the Bible, Exodus, picks up the same story centuries later. The original children of Israel had all died, but their progeny flourished. The people of God had become as numerous as the stars in the heavens, precisely as God promised Abraham. Unfortunately, this flourishing caused the Egyptians to fear their numbers and their loyalty. And by this time, Egypt had also forgotten about Joseph and how he had saved them from devastation so long ago. The Egyptians enslaved Israel's children, and the new Pharaoh instituted a barbaric form of population control: "Throw every newborn Hebrew boy into the Nile River. But you may let the girls live" (Exodus 1:22).

We can see the meticulous long view of God's plans as this story unfolds. And we can also see the formidable opposition to the promise of a people set apart.

In our world of instant gratification, we can barely comprehend the idea of a promise from God that will not be accomplished in our lifetimes—much less centuries later. But as we look back on the story of Scripture thus far, we see God's foresight and intentionality with the children of Israel.

First, God promised to Abraham a land and descendants without number. God revealed Himself to Abraham's son of promise, Isaac, who passed the promise to Jacob. God then revealed Himself to Jacob, who passed this promise to his twelve sons. And although it had been centuries and the people were enslaved far away from this Promised Land, the promise remained.

When the children of Israel began to cry out, God heard. A baby boy was put into the Nile as commanded, but he was placed in the river within a wicker basket. This wicker basket was discovered by Pharaoh's daughter, and the boy was given the name Moses. We'll get to know him very well in the coming weeks.

PRAYER:
Rise up, O LORD, in all your power. With music and singing we celebrate your mighty acts.   PSALM 21:13

JANUARY 26 · *day 26*

Exodus 2:11–3:22; Matthew 17:10-27; Psalm 22:1-18; Proverbs 5:7-14

MOSES GREW UP with an identity crisis. We'll see that show up from time to time as we get to know him. He was rescued from drowning in the Nile River by Pharaoh's daughter and was partially raised by his own mother. He was ethnically Hebrew—a slave—but was treated and educated like an Egyptian royal. This internal conflict led to his downfall in today's reading. Moses murdered an Egyptian, and the next day, his fellow Hebrews ridiculed him for it. When Pharaoh was informed, he wanted to kill Moses, which forced Moses to run for his life.

Eventually, Moses settled in a distant land and pursued a new life. He married and became a shepherd—until God stepped in. One day, Moses saw a bush that was aflame but was not being consumed.

> *"Moses!" God said from the bush, startling Moses.[3]*
> *"Here I am!" Moses replied.*   Exodus 3:4

This simple exchange encapsulates a posture that we absolutely must master if we are to truly find stability and comfort in our faith journey. This simple call-and-response is a massive turning point in the Bible. We're certainly still following the story of a people set apart and a Promised Land that began with Abraham. But the story is about to move into high gear—and it all began with a simple response: "Here I am!"

The ensuing conversation between God and Moses revealed that the cry of the people had been heard and that God was on the move. Moses was instructed to return to Egypt and inform the people. He was then to demand the release of the Hebrews from Pharaoh himself.

Moses argued that the Hebrew people would never believe such a thing—and that they would certainly not believe in Moses as the messenger. "Who am I supposed to tell them sent me?" he asked (Exodus 3:13).[4]

"I AM WHO I AM," was God's reply.

When the Great I Am calls, let's be paying attention. Whenever we answer His call, freedom is directly in front of us.

PRAYER:
You brought me safely from my mother's womb and led me to trust you at my mother's breast. I was thrust into your arms at my birth. You have been my God from the moment I was born.   PSALM 22:9-10

---

[3] Author's paraphrase.
[4] Author's paraphrase.

JANUARY 27 · *day 27*

Exodus 4:1–5:21; Matthew 18:1-20; Psalm 22:19-31; Proverbs 5:15-21

YESTERDAY, WE NOTICED that Moses had reservations about God's instructions to return to Egypt. In today's reading from Exodus, we continued with the conversation between Moses and God, and we encountered another of the saddest scenes in the Bible.

Moses explained to God why he was the wrong person, pleading that no one would believe him. God provided miraculous signs to solve this problem, but Moses wasn't finished with excuses. "O Lord, I'm not very good with words," he said. "I never have been, and I'm not now, even though you have spoken to me. I get tongue-tied, and my words get tangled" (Exodus 4:10).

How did God respond?

Who makes a person's mouth? Who decides whether people speak or do not speak, hear or do not hear, see or do not see? Is it not I, the LORD? Now go! I will be with you as you speak, and I will instruct you in what to say.
Exodus 4:11-12

This brings us to a very sad statement from the lips of Moses: "Lord, please! Send anyone else" (Exodus 4:13).

Through this exchange, once again, the Bible becomes a mirror into our souls. We've all done this in one way or another. In thought, word, or deed, we've explained to God why we are the wrong person and are not equipped to obey Him. We've all said, "Please send someone else," fully exposing our fears. This response also exposes the frailty of our faith. And yet "it is impossible to please God without faith" (Hebrews 11:6), and it is impossible to know God without faith.

In Matthew's Gospel, Jesus said, "I tell you the truth, unless you turn from your sins and become like little children, you will never get into the Kingdom of Heaven. . . . And anyone who welcomes a little child like this on my behalf is welcoming me" (Matthew 18:3, 5). We must reach higher than our highest reasoning and beyond our greatest fears to have the faith of a child who believes that all things are possible. Otherwise, we will mimic Moses and ask God to send someone else.

Thankfully, Moses ran out of excuses and returned to Egypt. The Bible would be quite a different story had he not. As with Joseph's story, things only got worse once Moses obeyed God. The slavery intensified, making everyone frustrated and angry with Moses. But as we shall soon see, God will not be thwarted.

WORSHIP:

All who seek the LORD will praise him. Their hearts will rejoice with everlasting joy. The whole earth will acknowledge the LORD and return to him. All the families of the nations will bow down before him. For royal power belongs to the LORD. He rules all the nations. PSALM 22:26-28

JANUARY 28 · *day 28*

Exodus 5:22–7:25; Matthew 18:21–19:12; Psalm 23:1-6; Proverbs 5:22-23

TODAY, THE BOOK of Proverbs told us, "An evil man is held captive by his own sins; they are ropes that catch and hold him" (Proverbs 5:22). The overwhelming truth of this proverb will unfold before us in our next chapters from Exodus, as the Egyptian pharaoh stands in the way of God's plan to free the children of Israel from slavery.

As we look to Matthew's Gospel, we read Jesus' words on a topic that He relentlessly kept in focus. Peter asked Him, "Lord, how often should I forgive someone who sins against me? Seven times?" Jesus replied, "No, not seven times . . . but seventy times seven!" (Matthew 18:21-22).

To illustrate the profound implications of withholding forgiveness, Jesus told the story of a man who was in debt to his king, more than he could ever pay. To satisfy the debt, the man was to be sold, along with his wife, children, and possessions. The money from this sale would go to the king in repayment. The man fell before the king and begged for more time—and then the king did something completely unexpected: He forgave the debt in its entirety. He gave the man his life back.

As the newly liberated man left the palace, he ran into another man who owed him a much smaller amount of money. He demanded payment and would not relent, throwing this poor man into prison until the debt could be paid.

When the king found out, he immediately summoned the man to whom he had forgiven a fortune. "You evil servant!" he said. "I forgave you that tremendous debt because you pleaded with me. Shouldn't you have mercy on your fellow servant, just as I had mercy on you?" (Matthew 18:32-33).

The man was thrown into prison until he could repay the entire debt. And, according to Jesus, "That's what my heavenly Father will do to you if you refuse to forgive your brothers and sisters from your heart" (Matthew 18:35).

Forgiveness is not optional in God's Kingdom. There is no way to walk intimately with God while unforgiveness is eating us from within like a cancer.

PRAYER:

The LORD is my shepherd; I have all that I need. He lets me rest in green meadows; he leads me beside peaceful streams. He renews my strength. He guides me along right paths, bringing honor to his name. Even when I walk through the darkest valley, I will not be afraid, for you are close beside me. Your rod and your staff protect and comfort me. You prepare a feast for me in the presence of my enemies. You honor me by anointing my head with oil. My cup overflows with blessings. Surely your goodness and unfailing love will pursue me all the days of my life, and I will live in the house of the LORD forever.   PSALM 23

JANUARY 29 · *day 29*

Exodus 8:1–9:35; Matthew 19:13-30; Psalm 24:1-10; Proverbs 6:1-5

TODAY IN EXODUS, plagues began to devastate the Egyptians. Pharaoh had been warned, and God had given signs, but Pharaoh could not conceive of a God higher than himself and the gods of Egypt. The Nile River—their source of fresh water—was turned to blood; frogs invaded the land; gnats swarmed and infested Egypt; flies pestered and contaminated the countryside, and the Egyptian livestock died. Boils began breaking out on the bodies of the Egyptian population, and legendary hail fell from the sky, destroying their crops.

At each turn, Pharaoh summoned Moses and begged for relief, but when God removed each plague, Pharaoh became stubborn and refused to allow the children of Israel their freedom.

In our reading in Matthew today, a rich young ruler asked Jesus an important question: "Teacher, what good deed must I do to have eternal life?" (Matthew 19:16).

Jesus' response was that the man should obey the commandments, to which the man replied that all his life, he had indeed obeyed them.

"If you want to be perfect," Jesus said, "go and sell all your possessions and give the money to the poor, and you will have treasure in heaven. Then come, follow me" (Matthew 19:21). The man departed in sadness because he was very wealthy.

In this encounter, we saw Jesus moving behind what was on the surface and into matters of the heart—where the truth lives. Jesus invited the rich man to rid himself of the one thing that gave him status and security, the one thing that was more important to him than God. And in the process, Jesus invited him to "come, follow me."

In the words of Jesus here, we find opportunity to examine our own hearts. What things are we valuing more than our relationship with God? As stark as this question is, these are the idols in our lives. And in this story, we realize once again that a true life of faith is an all-or-nothing proposition—a theme that we'll notice distinctly as we journey deeper into the Gospels.

WORSHIP:
Open up, ancient gates! Open up, ancient doors, and let the King of glory enter. Who is the King of glory? The LORD, strong and mighty; the LORD, invincible in battle. Open up, ancient gates! Open up, ancient doors, and let the King of glory enter. Who is the King of glory? The LORD of Heaven's Armies—he is the King of glory. PSALM 24:7-10

JANUARY 30 · *day 30*

Exodus 10:1–12:13; Matthew 20:1-28; Psalm 25:1-15; Proverbs 6:6-11

THE PLAGUES VISITED on the Egyptians continued in Exodus today. After all that Egypt had endured, Pharaoh's advisors were getting the message loud and clear. "Don't you realize that Egypt lies in ruins?" they asked Pharaoh (Exodus 10:7). But he would not be humiliated in front of his people. His pride was destroying the nation of Egypt, but he would not humble himself in the face of the overwhelmingly powerful God of the Hebrews. So locusts came in swarms that covered all of Egypt, and in the aftermath, "not a single leaf was left on the trees and plants throughout the land of Egypt" (Exodus 10:15).

Once again, Pharaoh feigned humility, and the plague was removed—and Pharaoh's heart hardened.

Next, a plague of darkness fell upon the land. And once again, Pharaoh attempted to negotiate a deal that would keep ties between the enslaved Hebrews and the Egyptians. But God sought total emancipation for his people. An enraged Pharaoh told Moses, "I'm warning you. Never come back to see me again! The day you see my face, you will die!"

"Very well," Moses replied. "I will never see your face again" (Exodus 10:28-29).

In Matthew's Gospel, Jesus continued to lay out the fundamentals of how God's Kingdom works and the postures we must maintain to observe it in action. "You know that the rulers in this world lord it over their people, and officials flaunt their authority over those under them," Jesus said. "But among you it will be different. Whoever wants to be a leader among you must be your servant, and whoever wants to be first among you must become your slave. For even the Son of Man came not to be served but to serve others and to give his life as a ransom for many" (Matthew 20:25-28).

Jesus' life and teachings are diametrically opposed to the attitudes and actions of a person like Pharaoh. And yet, we can find the postures of pride and arrogance in our own lives quite easily. Jesus invites us to look at our purpose in terms of how we can help people who need help, pretty much in any context. May we invite the Holy Spirit today to show us the relief of reaching outward and the joy of serving.

PRAYER:

O Lᴏʀᴅ, I give my life to you. I trust in you, my God! . . . Show me the right path, O Lᴏʀᴅ; point out the road for me to follow. Lead me by your truth and teach me, for you are the God who saves me. All day long I put my hope in you. PSALM 25:1-2, 4-5

JANUARY 31 · *day 31*

Exodus 12:14–13:16; Matthew 20:29–21:22; Psalm 25:16-22; Proverbs 6:12-15

THE COUNSEL OF the Proverbs today perfectly describes Pharaoh's behavior in Exodus: "Their perverted hearts plot evil, and they constantly stir up trouble. But they will be destroyed suddenly, broken in an instant beyond all hope of healing" (Proverbs 6:14-15).

After the plague of darkness, it would only take one final act to break the chains that had enslaved the children of Israel—but the last plague would be devastating. Moses instructed God's people to observe the first Passover, in which they painted blood on their doorposts so that a death angel would "pass over" their homes while invading Egypt. But wailing and bitter grief swept across Egypt as the firstborn son in every other household died, including the firstborn of Pharaoh.

"Get out!" Pharaoh ordered Moses. "Leave my people—and take the rest of the Israelites with you! Go and worship the LORD as you have requested. Take your flocks and herds, as you said, and be gone. Go, but bless me as you leave" (Exodus 12:31-32).

Immediately, the children of Israel began moving out of Egypt to the east, into the desert. On their way, they received anything they asked for, thereby pillaging the Egyptians' wealth as they left the country. Over a million people began a long journey, and as we concluded our first month of this amazing journey through the Bible this year, we saw the people of God reach another major mile marker: freedom. The promise to Abraham, Isaac, and Jacob was taking shape in new and fascinating ways. The people were now as vast as the stars in the heavens, but their entire identity would need to shift before they reached the Promised Land.

In Matthew today, Jesus said, "I tell you the truth, if you have faith and don't doubt, you can do things like this and much more. You can even say to this mountain, 'May you be lifted up and thrown into the sea,' and it will happen. You can pray for anything, and if you have faith, you will receive it" (Matthew 21:21-22).

The faith required in the Exodus of the children of Israel was the same faith required in the life of Jesus—and the same faith required in our own lives. We have an unfathomably powerful and sovereign heavenly Father. When we put our complete faith and trust in Him, anything is possible.

PRAYER:
Turn to me and have mercy, for I am alone and in deep distress. My problems go from bad to worse. Oh, save me from them all! Feel my pain and see my trouble. Forgive all my sins. . . . Do not let me be disgraced, for in you I take refuge. May integrity and honesty protect me, for I put my hope in you.   PSALM 25:16-18, 20-21

MAY 1 · *day 121*

Judges 13:1–14:20; John 1:29-51; Psalm 102:1-28; Proverbs 14:15-16

AS WE EMBARK on a new month, and the changing of seasons comes into full bloom, we begin the fascinating story of Samson, one of Israel's judges. As his story unfolds, we'll get not only a glimpse into the volatile times the children of Israel were navigating but also a good, hard look into our own souls. Samson will teach us much in the days ahead.

In John's Gospel, we found ourselves back at the Jordan River, as Jesus began His ministry and a loose band of brothers began to coalesce around Him. It is truly fascinating how Jesus chose His inner circle. There were no job interviews, no reviews of education and work experience. He wasn't looking for the smartest or strongest people He could find. He didn't pick anyone with marketing experience or hire a speechwriter. His invitation was accessible to all with an open heart and ears ready to hear. Jesus chose ill-equipped people who went on to change the world. And He still does. You are one of them.

Today in Psalm 102, the imagery of despair and struggle is exquisite, speaking of things we've all felt at one point or another:

> *My days disappear like smoke, and my bones burn like red-hot coals. My heart is sick, withered like grass, and I have lost my appetite. . . . I am reduced to skin and bones. . . . I lie awake, lonely as a solitary bird on the roof. . . . I eat ashes for food. My tears run down into my drink. . . . My life passes as swiftly as the evening shadows. I am withering away like grass.* Psalm 102:3-5, 7, 9, 11

As we ponder the plight of the writer, we may realize that we've experienced these seasons as well. If we choose to stay in that place of despair, depression and hopelessness will obviously soon follow. But that's not where the psalmist stayed:

> *Let this be recorded for future generations, so that a people not yet born will praise the LORD. Tell them the LORD looked down from his heavenly sanctuary. He looked down to earth from heaven to hear the groans of the prisoners, to release those condemned to die.* Psalm 102:18-20

Amid suffering, the psalmist found hope. But in that hope, he looked forward to future generations. This psalm was certainly a cry of the heart, but it was written for you. You are a part of those "future generations." The psalmist told us that God rescued him, and his witness is calling to us across time so that we might remember. Let's take comfort in knowing that the Scriptures are speaking directly to us today with hope. We are God's children, and we "will thrive in [His] presence" (Psalm 102:28).

MEDITATION:

You are always the same; you will live forever. The children of your people will live in security. Their children's children will thrive in your presence.   PSALM 102:27-28

MAY 2 · day 122

Judges 15:1–16:31; John 2:1-25; Psalm 103:1-22; Proverbs 14:17-19

SAMSON WAS UNIQUE from birth. He was a Nazirite, which means he was set apart for God's service (Judges 13:5). He was never to drink alcohol, eat forbidden food, or have his hair cut. Because of this, he had unparalleled strength.

During Samson's life, the Philistines had ruled over Israel for forty years. The conflict between the Philistines and Samson arose because of one primary issue: women. At first, Samson created a wager and a riddle to enrich himself and his anticipated new life with his Philistine fiancée. Unfortunately, she betrayed him and gave the answer away. Samson retaliated by killing Philistines. Obviously, this didn't sit well with the Philistine people. When Samson cooled off and went to retrieve his wife, he discovered that she had been given to another man. Enraged, Samson burned Philistine crops. Again, this didn't sit well with the Philistine people, but they couldn't capture and kill Samson—he was too strong for them.

Eventually, Samson met the infamous Delilah. After much manipulation, Samson told Delilah the true source of his strength, and she betrayed him. The Philistines cut his hair, the Spirit of God that had surrounded him left, and he was captured and blinded. The great Israelite warrior became a circus act of sorts for the Philistines. They enslaved him and publicly humiliated him without noticing that his hair was slowly growing back.

The Philistines brought Samson to the temple of the Philistine god, Dagon, amid a massive festival. As the party turned into a drunken celebration, the people worshiped Dagon for giving them victory over their greatest enemy. Samson's life ended with a prayer: "Sovereign LORD, remember me again. O God, please strengthen me just one more time" (Judges 16:28).

With that prayer, Samson pushed against the temple pillars, bringing the roof down on top of himself and destroying it, along with those inside.

Like Samson, all of God's people are set apart. And like Samson, all of God's people sin. But there is a powerful reminder in Samson's story. Despite Samson's sinful flaws, God never abandoned His servant—it was the other way around.

When Samson prayed during the final moments of his life, the Lord answered and gave him the strength he needed to once again defeat Israel's enemies.

WORSHIP:
Let all that I am praise the LORD; with my whole heart, I will praise his holy name. Let all that I am praise the LORD; may I never forget the good things he does for me. He forgives all my sins and heals all my diseases. He redeems me from death and crowns me with love and tender mercies. He fills my life with good things. My youth is renewed like the eagle's!
PSALM 103:1-5

MAY 3 · *day 123*

Judges 17:1–18:31; John 3:1-21; Psalm 104:1-23; Proverbs 14:20-21

TODAY, WE READ perhaps the most famous of all Scriptures in John 3:16: "For God so loved the world . . ." (ESV).

We can each probably quote it from memory. What may be less known is its context. Before it became a famous verse, it was part of a conversation. Jesus said the words about His Father as part of a broader discussion with a religious leader named Nicodemus, who had come under the cover of darkness to speak with Him. Jesus said that Nicodemus would never see the Kingdom of God unless he was born again. Nicodemus responded with obvious confusion.

This short conversation is essentially the heart of the gospel. Jesus told Nicodemus that there is a physical birth (of water) and a spiritual birth (of spirit) (John 3:5). "The Holy Spirit gives birth to spiritual life" (John 3:6), and this spiritual life is eternal. This is what being "born again" means: the reintegration of the Spirit of God within a human being.

"For this is how God loved the world," Jesus said. "He gave his one and only Son, so that everyone who believes in him will not perish but have eternal life" (John 3:16).

Our pure-hearted belief in Jesus alters the trajectory of our lives and awakens new life within us, and our true affirmation of this fact opens our hearts to God's Spirit within.

"God sent his Son into the world not to judge the world, but to save the world through him," Jesus continued. "There is no judgment against anyone who believes in him. But anyone who does not believe in him has already been judged for not believing in God's one and only Son. And the judgment is based on this fact: God's light came into the world, but people loved the darkness more than the light, for their actions were evil. All who do evil hate the light and refuse to go near it for fear their sins will be exposed" (John 3:17-20).

That last paragraph, straight from Jesus' lips, gives us much to contemplate. Those who truly believe have no judgment against them. Anyone who does not believe is already experiencing judgment. It's easy enough to see this reality in the world. People love the darkness more than the light because the light exposes the truth about them.

What are you afraid of having exposed? That is what is pulling you toward the darkness. Invite the eternal Spirit of God that Jesus spoke of in John 3 today to shine the light of truth within you, for it is the truth that will set you free (John 8:32).

MEDITATION:
It is a sin to belittle one's neighbor; blessed are those who help the poor.
PROVERBS 14:21

MAY 4 · day 124

Judges 19:1–20:48; John 3:22–4:3; Psalm 104:24-35; Proverbs 14:22-24

HAVE YOU EVER gotten excited about starting a new chapter in your life? Maybe you've decided to finally go back to school and finish that degree. Or perhaps you're going to sit down and finally write that memoir. Maybe you want to radically change your health and have decided to train for a marathon. The decision to act is tremendously empowering and inspiring.

You set a date to begin, and you can't stop thinking or talking about it. You shop for all the things you believe will create the perfect creative environment, or maybe you spend hours reading all the reviews of the best long-distance running shoes. You can barely sleep the night before you begin this new journey.

Then the day arrives, and reality sets in about ten minutes later—this is going to be a long journey, full of very, very hard work. All those books on writing were inspiring to read in preparation, but for some reason, the blank page in front of you won't write itself. All that shopping for a stylish workout wardrobe and shoes won't increase endurance or burn calories, so you find yourself plopped in front of the television that evening with a bag of chips, feeling defeated, because the idea of accomplishing something new was far more enticing than actually doing it.

This is addressed in our reading from Proverbs today: "Work brings profit, but mere talk leads to poverty!" (Proverbs 14:23).

The words *profit* and *poverty* in this passage are not referring only to financial status. Rather, they refer to abundance and lack. In other words, talking about doing something does not get it done. Planning to do something does not complete it. Reading a book on writing will not make you a writer, and buying the right running shoes will not make you a runner. It is the work involved—the sweat of the thing—that moves you from desire and lack to fulfillment and abundance. This truth touches all places in our lives, including our relationship with God. Desiring to know God and reading books about God will not create intimacy with God, any more than it would with a spouse or loved one. The work is what brings the abundance.

What are the things you need to stop talking about and start working on? Invite God into that question today.

O LORD, what a variety of things you have made! In wisdom you have made them all. The earth is full of your creatures.   PSALM 104:24

MAY 5 · *day 125*

Judges 21:1–Ruth 1:22; John 4:4-42; Psalm 105:1-15; Proverbs 14:25

TODAY, WE COMPLETED the book of Judges and began the book of Ruth—and it couldn't come at a better time. After witnessing the chaotic extremes of rebellion and the challenging leadership of the judges at critical moments in the development of the Israelites, Ruth comes like a refreshing breeze and begins transitioning us into the next season for God's people.

Ruth is the story of three people who chose to do the right thing despite hard and bitter circumstances. This book shows us that when people of character make correct decisions, God's faithfulness is ever present. It also gives us a beautiful portrait of valiant women of character. Because of Ruth's and Naomi's faithfulness, King David would be born—and through the line of David, Jesus would come.

In John's Gospel, Jesus visited the Samaritan people and revealed again how counterintuitively God's Kingdom operates.

"You know the saying, 'One plants and another harvests,'" Jesus said. "And it's true. I sent you to harvest where you didn't plant; others had already done the work, and now you will get to gather the harvest" (John 4:37-38).

In our culture, we plant or invest or work to reap the benefit of our labor. In God's Kingdom, things are a little different. Sometimes, we plant seeds of faith in someone's life but will never see the outcome. Later, someone else may reap the harvest of what we've planted. At other times, we will reap the harvest that someone else planted. We're all in this together. Or in Jesus' words, "The harvesters are paid good wages, and the fruit they harvest is people brought to eternal life. What joy awaits both the planter and the harvester alike!" (John 4:36).

Understand that you are planting seeds wherever you go and in whatever you do today. And those seeds will yield a harvest, whether you ever see it or not. But also remember that when you are there to witness the rebirth of a soul, someone else planted the seeds you are harvesting. Every piece of it matters—whether we plant or harvest. And there is great joy in laboring for the Kingdom.

WORSHIP:

Give thanks to the LORD and proclaim his greatness. Let the whole world know what he has done. Sing to him; yes, sing his praises. Tell everyone about his wonderful deeds. Exult in his holy name; rejoice, you who worship the LORD.   PSALM 105:1-3

MAY 6 · *day 126*

Ruth 2:1–4:22; John 4:43-54; Psalm 105:16-36; Proverbs 14:26-27

RUTH WAS A Moabite woman, and her mother-in-law, Naomi, was a Hebrew. Their fates brought them together because of loss. Naomi's husband and two sons died in the land of Moab, which left her a widow in a foreign land—a bitter pill to swallow, indeed. One of those sons happened to be the husband of Ruth, and when Naomi decided to take her bitterness and return to her homeland, Ruth would not leave her. This allegiance was remarkable, for Ruth was leaving everything behind to devote her life to Naomi.

When they arrived back in Israel, Ruth's story of devotion carried great weight among the Hebrew people. But a good reputation doesn't always put food on the table, and Ruth began working in fields, gathering what was left or dropped by the harvesters. Allowing widows and orphans to gather what they could in this way was commanded in the Mosaic law (Leviticus 23:22).

Naomi soon discovered that Ruth had been working in the fields belonging to a close relative named Boaz. The traditional site of these fields can still be seen near Bethlehem today. Boaz was incredibly kind to Ruth as she gleaned from his fields, and before long, the wise Naomi took note of his kindness. She guided Ruth through the process of signifying her availability to Boaz while retaining her dignity, and it worked. Boaz and Ruth were married shortly thereafter, and when Ruth conceived and gave birth to a son named Obed, Naomi's grief and bitterness were replaced by joy. Obed would later become a father himself. His son's name was Jesse, and Jesse would one day become the father of King David.

It is beautiful how God arranged the lives of Ruth, Boaz, and Naomi; how He turned famine, death, and loss into abundance, joy, and redemption. In this story, we see heartbreak and bitterness. But we also see how character, dignity, loyalty, and trust in God lead toward new life, rather than further into darkness. No matter the bitterness we are facing now, our story is not completed. If we choose to be people of character and faith, we will be following the path of Ruth, Naomi, and Boaz—and remarkable good can come from tremendous hardship.

MEDITATION:

Those who fear the LORD are secure; he will be a refuge for their children.   PROVERBS 14:26

MAY 7 · *day 127*

1 Samuel 1:1–2:21; John 5:1-23; Psalm 105:37-45; Proverbs 14:28-29

TODAY, WE BEGAN moving into a new era in the story of God's people as we launched into the book of 1 Samuel. We'll first learn about Samuel's remarkable story and calling. But Samuel will eventually lead us to Israel's first monarch—Saul. In Saul, we'll find a great deal of challenging parallels to our own lives. Later, we'll meet a man named David. Of course, we've been getting to know David through his poetry and songs, found in the Psalms, but his life will also teach us remarkable things about ourselves.

We'll be spending a fair amount of time within these stories, so this is a good time to provide ourselves with a little context. A good number of scholars believe that the material contained in the books of Samuel were originally recorded by three prophets of Israel: Samuel, Nathan, and Gad. Originally, 1 and 2 Samuel were not written as separate texts but were grouped together with 1 and 2 Kings as a continuous text.

When the Old Testament was translated into Greek—which is called the Septuagint—the books were divided into four separate texts known as the Books of the Kingdoms. Later, when the Old Testament was translated into Latin—called the Vulgate—they became the Books of the Kings. At that time, the texts were known as 1, 2, 3, and 4 Kings.

Confused? Stay with me, because it can be a bit complicated.

What is now known as 1 and 2 Samuel was actually 1 and 2 Kings in the Latin translations. This all finally changed to the currently accepted books of Samuel and Kings when translators created the King James Bible in 1611.

Samuel became a very influential person. He was the final judge of Israel, but he was also a prophet of God and served before the Lord as priest. During his life, everyone was doing what was right in their own eyes. Samuel stepped into this breach as a prophet and alleviated some of the anarchy for one simple reason: Samuel was speaking directly for God, and that was something the children of Israel took seriously at the time, for this was how Moses had led them.

Buckle up. We're in for a fantastic ride through a season of great transition in the story of our spiritual ancestors.

MEDITATION:
People with understanding control their anger; a hot temper shows great foolishness.   PROVERBS 14:29

MAY 8 · *day 128*

1 Samuel 2:22–4:22; John 5:24-47; Psalm 106:1-12; Proverbs 14:30-31

OUR READING TODAY provided a lot to ruminate on.

The story in 1 Samuel told us of Samuel's calling and rise to prominence amid the unethical behavior of his brethren in the Tabernacle at Shiloh. Eli was the high priest at the time, and he had grown old and fat. Eli's sons were to be the next generation of priests, but they were busy pilfering the best of the sacrificial food and having sex with the women who assisted at the Tabernacle. God called Samuel away from this example, and his first prophetic word was a difficult judgment on Eli and his sons. This judgment came true shortly thereafter: The Philistines captured the Ark of the Covenant in battle, Eli's sons were killed in the same battle, and Eli fell over and broke his neck when he received the news.

119

In John's Gospel, Jesus spoke words that are clear and direct:

I tell you the truth, those who listen to my message and believe in God who sent me have eternal life. They will never be condemned for their sins, but they have already passed from death into life. John 5:24

The implications of this truth in our lives are profound. Those of us who listen to Jesus' words and believe in the God who sent His Son will never be condemned for sin—ever. This is unspeakably good news. This is precisely the Good News that we are to be living in and spreading to the ends of the earth.

Our reading from Proverbs today spoke practically about our health: "A peaceful heart leads to a healthy body" (Proverbs 14:30). Often, the stresses of life send us toward the medical community, where we seek a pill to cure our ills or a procedure to correct what has begun failing. Although science and medicine are beautiful gifts from God, intentionally seeking peace within is a preventative medicine that is always available and can profoundly affect our health.

The proverb goes on to say, "Jealousy is like cancer in the bones" (Proverbs 14:30). This is kind of a big deal. The Bible is equating rivalry, vengeful competition, resentment, and suspicion to cancer. And who signs up to have cancer?

Choosing to constantly compare our lives to others in the pursuit of identity and superiority is like signing up to have cancer. Invite the Holy Spirit into jealous areas in your life. According to the Bible, those things are eating you alive—and if you stop to consider it, you can feel the truth in this. Thankfully, there is a cure. Ask God to show you what a peaceful heart looks, feels, and acts like today, as you release the cancer of jealousy that will only kill you in the end.

WORSHIP:
Praise the LORD! Give thanks to the LORD, for he is good! His faithful love endures forever. Who can list the glorious miracles of the LORD? Who can ever praise him enough? PSALM 106:1-2

MAY 9 · *day 129*

1 Samuel 5:1–7:17; John 6:1-21; Psalm 106:13-31; Proverbs 14:32-33

THE LOSS OF the Ark of the Covenant to the Philistines demoralized the children of Israel. But the Philistines didn't have an easy time of it either. At first, it seemed as if the Philistine god Dagon had defeated the God of the Hebrews. The Ark was transported to Dagon's temple in one of the five major capital cities of Philistia: Ashdod. Ashdod sits on the Mediterranean coast and still exists today. After the arrival of the Ark, Dagon's statue was found facedown before the Ark on two consecutive mornings, and then skin tumors began breaking out among the people.

In fear for their lives, the leaders decided to transport the Ark inland to Gath, another of their capital cities. The ruins of Gath also exist today and continue to be excavated. Gath was the hometown of the giant Goliath. Unfortunately, those living in and around Gath suffered the same outbreak of skin tumors.

Next, the Ark was taken north to Ekron—yet another of the great Philistine cities that remain as an archaeological site. But the people there were terrified of what Yahweh might do to them. They begged that the Ark be returned to the Hebrew people, and that is what happened. The Philistines prepared a guilt offering made of gold reliefs of their tumors, as well as golden rats, and loaded the Ark onto a cart, sending it away. They reasoned that if the cattle pulling the cart returned to Israel, then it was in fact the God of Israel who was angry with them. The cows went straight back into Israeli territory, ending their journey at Beth-shemesh, which also still exists and is undergoing continued archaeological study.

Obviously, the people of Beth-shemesh were overjoyed to receive this national treasure and emblem of their heritage and relationship with the Lord—but this joy was short-lived. After multiple sacrifices, seventy men looked inside the Ark and died.

"'Who is able to stand in the presence of the LORD, this holy God?' they cried out" (1 Samuel 6:20). The power of the almighty God was not something to be trifled with, and His commands were to be obeyed.

As grim as the situation was for both the Philistines and the inhabitants of Beth-shemesh, the entire episode solidified Samuel's leadership. Through that leadership, all the idol worship was cleansed from Israel, and the Philistines were subdued. The children of Israel had once again returned to the God who had called them out of Egypt and planted them in their homeland.

In Proverbs today, we learned that our hearts are shrines—sort of: "Wisdom is enshrined in an understanding heart" (Proverbs 14:33).

In other words, an understanding heart is a revered place for wisdom. Conversely, "Wisdom is not found among fools," Proverbs tells us (14:33). Foolishness (in thought, word, or deed) is not a place where wisdom thrives, and wisdom is what we need to grow deeper in intimacy with God.

Are you actively seeking out wisdom in your life? Is it important enough to have it enshrined in your heart? Like everything good in life, gaining wisdom will not happen by default. Wisdom is something we must actively seek and cultivate by the choices we make today and every day.

MEDITATION:
The wicked are crushed by disaster, but the godly have a refuge when they die. PROVERBS 14:32

MAY 10 · day 130

1 Samuel 8:1–9:27; John 6:22-42; Psalm 106:32-48; Proverbs 14:34-35

IN OUR OLD Testament reading today, we drew near to the end of Samuel's life. Samuel was the final judge of Israel, but this was not the original plan. Samuel had two sons of his own, and he appointed them as cojudges to take his place. Sadly, they did not walk in their father's footsteps. Instead, they perverted justice and used their authority to exact bribes.

Knowing that time was crucial, the elders of Israel discussed the matter with Samuel: "'Look,' they told him, 'you are now old, and your sons are not like you. Give us a king to judge us like all the other nations have'" (1 Samuel 8:5).

This is the backstory for how Israel moved into the era of monarchy. Samuel was displeased. God was displeased. But God instructed Samuel to honor their wishes, and today we met the man who would become the first king of Israel: Saul. But Saul's story speaks far beyond a historical account. His life mimics our own tendencies on many levels, and we should pay close attention, for the Bible will speak volumes in the coming weeks.

Speaking of diligent attention, Jesus had volumes to speak of his own in John's Gospel today: "This is the only work God wants from you: Believe in the one he has sent" (John 6:29).

This sentence alone should stop us. Because aren't we continually trying to figure out what God desires from us? According to Jesus, all God wants is for us to believe. Perhaps we've drastically overcomplicated things. Jesus' words are truly foundational to our lives. After all, it's hard to love someone you don't believe in. It's certainly impossible to have a relationship with someone you don't believe in. Maybe the foundational question is whether we truly believe in Jesus.

In response to Jesus' profoundly simple declaration, the people challenged Him: "Show us a miraculous sign if you want us to believe in you. What can you do?" (John 6:30).

This demand comes across as rather arrogant until we put the mirror before our own lives. Are we continually asking God to prove Himself to us? Are we offering our belief in exchange for some kind of benefit or sign? And if so, is that really unfettered belief and true love, or are we, like those people, asking, "What can you do?" Think on these things today, and invite Jesus to peel back the layers of why you follow Him.

MEDITATION:

Godliness makes a nation great, but sin is a disgrace to any people. PROVERBS 14:34

MAY 11 · *day 131*

1 Samuel 10:1–11:15; John 6:43-71; Psalm 107:1-43; Proverbs 15:1-3

SAUL HAD TAKEN a servant and set out to find lost donkeys. He had no idea that he would return the anointed king of Israel, but when he encountered Samuel, this is exactly what happened. Samuel anointed him with oil and gave him several prophetic words that all came true in succession. Then Samuel summoned the people of Israel to the town of Mizpah, which was near Saul's hometown of Gibeah; both towns were within view of Jerusalem.

With much fanfare, Samuel drew lots to systematically narrow down the chosen one before the people. When Saul was selected, he was nowhere to be found. "So they asked the LORD, 'Where is he?' And the LORD replied, 'He is hiding among the baggage'" (1 Samuel 10:22).

How often have we witnessed God's movement in our lives and felt called or chosen to participate, only to hide in our own baggage when the time to step forward arrives? We see that Saul indeed looks the part of his calling, but he also carries within himself a great flaw—the fear of other people. We each carry this flaw to some degree. Saul will show us where those roads lead and will offer us clear choices for our lives.

In John's Gospel, Jesus simply cleared the deck. After continually being challenged to prove Himself, He told the crowds surrounding Him that if they didn't eat His flesh and drink His blood, they could not have eternal life within them. This was obviously a poor marketing choice. But Jesus wasn't trying to build a fan base. He wasn't interested in the circus that had begun swirling around Him.

He clarified His teaching: "I live because of the living Father who sent me; in the same way, anyone who feeds on me will live because of me. I am the true bread that came down from heaven. Anyone who eats this bread will not die as your ancestors did" (John 6:57-58).

Jesus was showing the crowd that there can be no eternal life unless there is union with God—a oneness of being and collaborative intertwining that we would otherwise call a truly life-giving relationship. But the people left in droves. Even some who had become close followers of Jesus abandoned Him.

As the crowds were slinking away, Jesus continued: "The Spirit alone gives eternal life. Human effort accomplishes nothing. And the very words I have spoken to you are spirit and life. But some of you do not believe me" (John 6:63-64).

It's a rather sobering and tragic scene to watch. The people heard the truth and walked away from God. Jesus turned to his twelve disciples. "Are you also going to leave?" He asked (John 6:67).

Simon Peter responded to Jesus' question, and his words must deeply and truly become our own: "Lord, to whom would we go? You have the words that give eternal life. We believe, and we know you are the Holy One of God" (John 6:68-69).

Jesus was never interested in forming a fan club. He still isn't. His message has a cost: everything. All that we are without Him. Union with God is something that will burn to ashes everything else. But in that burning is a rebirth, and that rebirth is eternal. The crowds left Jesus because they did not have ears to hear or eyes to see. Are we the same? What are the thoughts and intents of our hearts really saying about Jesus? Because in Him, union with God is not only possible—it's eternal.

MEDITATION:
Give thanks to the LORD, for he is good! His faithful love endures forever. Has the LORD redeemed you? Then speak out! Tell others he has redeemed you from your enemies.   PSALM 107:1-2

MAY 12 · *day 132*

1 Samuel 12:1–13:23; John 7:1-30; Psalm 108:1-13; Proverbs 15:4

YESTERDAY WE FOUND Saul hiding in the baggage at his own coronation. This revealed that Saul had a genuine fear of what people thought about him, a fear that had the potential to negatively color his decision making and leadership. In today's reading, we saw this fear again—to great consequence.

The Israelites now had a king, and they expected that king to begin delivering them from oppression—especially from the Philistines. Saul's son Jonathan had stirred the hornet's nest by attacking a Philistine garrison, and the Philistines brought a horde to retaliate and crush Israel.

Samuel told Saul to wait for him in Gilgal so that God could be invited to battle for his people, but after waiting an entire week, the Israelite army became terrified and began deserting Saul. So Saul decided to offer the sacrifice himself, a choice that cost him greatly. Samuel arrived as Saul was finishing and confronted him over his foolishness.

In his own defense, Saul said, "I saw my men scattering from me, and you didn't arrive when you said you would, and the Philistines are at Micmash ready for battle. So I said, 'The Philistines are ready to march against us at Gilgal, and I haven't even asked for the LORD's help!' So I felt compelled to offer the burnt offering myself before you came" (1 Samuel 13:11-12).

Saul's fear of circumstance and reputation cost him dearly. The kingdom was stripped from him in today's reading. It wouldn't happen immediately, but the damage was done. And we're given another clear view of what happens when our identity is carried by the tide of public opinion.

Our reading from Proverbs told us, "Gentle words are a tree of life; a deceitful tongue crushes the spirit" (Proverbs 15:4).

Notice that the proverb doesn't say that gentle words can make you feel kind of good—they are "a tree of life"! It doesn't say a deceitful tongue makes you feel a little bad—it "crushes" you! Clearly, the words we speak hold great weight in the Kingdom of God, for they have the power to be a tree of life—or to crush. Take some time to reflect on the language you use. Is it healing or crushing you and those around you?

WORSHIP:

My heart is confident in you, O God; no wonder I can sing your praises with all my heart! . . . For your unfailing love is higher than the heavens. Your faithfulness reaches to the clouds. Be exalted, O God, above the highest heavens. May your glory shine over all the earth.   PSALM 108:1, 4-5

MAY 13 · *day 133*

1 Samuel 14:1-52; John 7:31-53; Psalm 109:1-31; Proverbs 15:5-7

IN TODAY'S READING from 1 Samuel, Saul's son Jonathan covertly confronted a Philistine outpost, which successfully caused panic throughout the entire Philistine encampment, and the Philistines began attacking one another. When Saul saw what was happening, he made his men vow that they would not eat until they had taken vengeance on their enemies. Without nourishment, the men exhausted themselves, but Jonathan hadn't heard or taken this vow. He later learned of it, but not before eating from a honeycomb.

"'My father has made trouble for us all!' Jonathan exclaimed. 'A command like that only hurts us. See how refreshed I am now that I have eaten this little bit of honey'" (1 Samuel 14:29). Meanwhile, Israel's men circled back to the battlefield and ravenously began to kill and consume the livestock, due to hunger and exhaustion.

Saul wanted to chase the Philistines into the night and press the victory forward, but a priest suggested they consult with God on the matter. God had nothing to say.

"Something's wrong!" Saul exclaimed. "I want all my army commanders to come here. We must find out what sin was committed today. I vow by the name of the LORD who rescued Israel that the sinner will surely die, even if it is my own son Jonathan!" (1 Samuel 14:38-39).

Lots were drawn, and Jonathan was chosen as the offender.

"'Tell me what you have done,' Saul demanded of Jonathan.

"'I tasted a little honey,' Jonathan admitted. 'It was only a little bit on the end of my stick. Does that deserve death?'"

"'Yes, Jonathan,' Saul said, 'you must die! May God strike me and even kill me if you do not die for this'" (1 Samuel 14:43-44).

Obviously, Saul's reaction was incredibly harsh—especially with his own son, the prince of Israel and heir to the throne. But once again, we saw Saul's fear and insecurity navigate him into a drastic situation. However, the people would have nothing to do with it:

"Jonathan has won this great victory for Israel. Should he die? Far from it! As surely as the LORD lives, not one hair on his head will be touched, for God helped him do a great deed today" (1 Samuel 14:45).

Saul wanted to look the part of a strong and decisive leader, but he was plagued by deep issues of insecurity. This clouded his judgment and brought about what he greatly feared—humiliation before his people. His insecurity nearly cost Jonathan his life.

Has this been your story at times? Have you put yourself in situations where the only way was the wrong way, and you've had to face drastic consequences or humiliation because of bravado, pride, and insecurity? Invite God to speak about insecurity and the fear of others today. These must be rooted out of our lives if we seek clarity and wholeness.

PRAYER:

Help me, O LORD my God! Save me because of your unfailing love. Let them see that this is your doing, that you yourself have done it, LORD. Then let them curse me if they like, but you will bless me!   PSALM 109:26-28

MAY 14 · *day 134*

1 Samuel 15:1–16:23; John 8:1-20; Psalm 110:1-7; Proverbs 15:8-10

IN JOHN'S GOSPEL today, Jesus was teaching in the Temple complex in Jerusalem when the religious leaders put a humiliating test before Him. They had caught a woman in the act of adultery. In other words, they found a woman in bed, entangled with someone other than her husband, and dragged her off. They thrust her before Jesus—probably naked—to entrap Him.

"'Teacher,' they said to Jesus, 'this woman was caught in the act of adultery. The law of Moses says to stone her. What do you say?'" (John 8:4-5).

Jesus stooped down, and began writing in the dust. As He wrote, the crowd waited. When the religious leaders pressed Him for an answer, Jesus stood.

"All right," He said, "but let the one who has never sinned throw the first stone!" Then He stooped down again and wrote in the dust (John 8:7-8).

Slowly, the accusers dispersed. Jesus stood to face to the woman, joining her in her humiliation.

"Where are your accusers?" Jesus asked. "Didn't even one of them condemn you?"

"'No, Lord,' she said.

"And Jesus said, 'Neither do I. Go and sin no more'" (John 8:10-11).

The story is remarkably beautiful and has given hope for thousands of years. We are all the woman in this story in one way or another—we all have done things that deserve judgment. Ironically, we embrace the story for ourselves, claiming the grace given to the woman while often playing the role of the religious accusers toward others. All too often, we are willing to drag our brothers and sisters who have fallen in one way or another toward their judgment, while completely excusing our own shortcomings. Jesus didn't do that. He entered this woman's humiliation and set her free.

To be Christlike requires that we stop being merciful to ourselves while judging others. Jesus did not condemn the woman in this story. He acknowledged her and called her forward into a better life. May we remember that the words "Go and sin no more" do not apply only to us and our particular shortcomings. These words apply to everyone. The only one able to cast the first stone in this story was Jesus—He was the only one without sin. And He didn't. We must do the same if we want to be like Jesus.

MEDITATION:
What is more pleasing to the LORD: your burnt offerings and sacrifices or your obedience to his voice? Listen! Obedience is better than sacrifice, and submission is better than offering the fat of rams.   1 SAMUEL 15:22

MAY 15 · *day 135*

1 Samuel 17:1–18:4; John 8:21-30; Psalm 111:1-10; Proverbs 15:11

IN MODERN-DAY ISRAEL lies a narrow but fertile valley called Elah. On either side of the valley, hills quickly rise and cascade away. In ancient times, this valley was the borderland between Philistia and Israel, and it was within this valley that we spent our time in 1 Samuel today.

The Philistines encamped on one side of the valley, taunting the opposing Israelite army on the other side. The primary intimidation tactic for the Philistines was the voice of one of their warriors: Goliath. Every day, Goliath would walk into this valley and challenge the army of Israel to a man-to-man duel to the death that would decide the conflict between the two peoples. Each man would represent the entire army they came from, and the man who won would win for all.

Meanwhile, a young shepherd named David was sent by his father from his home near Bethlehem to bring supplies and check on his older brothers in the valley, about twelve miles away.

David arrived as the giant Goliath was giving his daily taunt. "Have you seen the giant?" the men asked. "He comes out each day to defy Israel. The king has offered a huge reward to anyone who kills him. He will give that man one of his daughters for a wife, and the man's entire family will be exempted from paying taxes!" (1 Samuel 17:25).

The offered reward was certainly appealing, but no man was willing to face Goliath—except the shepherd boy David. Before long, David was brought before King Saul, and David's youthful confidence, combined with his blind faith in God, convinced the king to allow him to face the giant.

Saul suited David in his own royal armor for the battle, but David couldn't fight this way. The armor didn't fit, and he wasn't accustomed to it—a good reminder for each of us to be who we are as we face trials and battles of our own. In the end, David went into the valley as he was—a shepherd boy who had killed lions and bears with nothing more than a deadly, accurate slingshot.

When Goliath saw a boy with no apparent weapon coming, he thought it was a joke. "Am I a dog," he roared at David, "that you come at me with a stick?" (1 Samuel 17:43).

But David had a reply ready, and this reply is what we must remember as we face our own giants:

> *You come to me with sword, spear, and javelin, but I come to you in the name of the LORD of Heaven's Armies—the God of the armies of Israel, whom you have defied. . . . And everyone assembled here will know that the LORD rescues his people, but not with sword and spear. This is the LORD's battle, and he will give you to us!* 1 Samuel 17:45, 47

David charged. A stone flew. The giant fell. And just like that, David went from total obscurity to a celebrated national hero. His life changed immediately, and his new popularity had a profound effect on a very insecure King Saul.

Thus far in 1 Samuel, we've been watching Saul's insecurities and fears consistently undermining his own leadership. From this point forward, David's and Saul's lives will be entangled, opening entirely new levels of paranoia and drama for Saul. But it will also offer dramatic opportunities for reflection on our own hearts' posture and motivations.

MEDITATION:
Even Death and Destruction hold no secrets from the LORD. How much more does he know the human heart! PROVERBS 15:11

MAY 16 · *day 136*

1 Samuel 18:5–19:24; John 8:31-59; Psalm 112:1-10; Proverbs 15:12-14

ANYTIME A KING comes to town, there is a crowd. Even today, when royalty or leaders of a nation visit, their arrival is on the news, and throngs of people congregate to get a glimpse. It was no different for King Saul when he returned victorious from battle—there was pageantry and celebration. But after David killed the giant Goliath, the song of the young women of Israel went like this: "Saul has killed his thousands, and David his ten thousands!" (1 Samuel 18:7).

"What's this?" Saul said. "They credit David with ten thousands and me with only thousands. Next they'll be making him their king!" (1 Samuel 18:8).

Saul's insecurity and jealousy only grew as time went on. In a rage, Saul tried to kill David with a spear, which David deftly avoided. Next, Saul sent David into battle, hoping he would be killed, but instead, David was successful. Then Saul invited David to marry his daughter Michal, setting the bride-price at a hundred Philistine foreskins—a grisly price indeed. But David did it. He presented the foreskins of two hundred Philistines to Saul. After that plan failed, Saul asked his son Jonathan—yes, the same Jonathan who Saul was going to kill for eating honey—to assassinate David, but Jonathan would not do it. So Saul attempted to kill David with a spear again—and missed again. Finally, Saul sent troops to David and Michal's house to assassinate him, but Michal helped him escape.

As Saul's insecurities mounted into a torrent of jealous paranoia, David continued to thrive, which only compounded Saul's issues. But David wasn't living large and flaunting his exploits. On the contrary, David had no choice but to grow up fast. He was thrust into celebrity with no prior training, and in the midst of it, he had to learn how to stay alive.

We can find ourselves in both men's lives. There are times when we shine—and times when we seem completely unmoored from ourselves. Both Saul and David knew who the God of Israel was. Both worshiped him. But Saul's insecurity and jealousy pulled him away from God, while David knew that God was his only hope for survival—as we often see in David's psalms.

These men's lives were irreversibly intertwined, but they were on completely divergent paths with God. We should pay close attention to where those paths lead as we move forward.

Our insecurities can only continue to plague us and will eventually cause chaos and destruction in our lives. Or we can choose another path—one of total and utter dependence on God for all that we have and are. Which path are you on? It's never too late to change course.

MEDITATION:
How joyful are those who fear the LORD and delight in obeying his commands. Their children will be successful everywhere; an entire generation of godly people will be blessed. PSALM 112:1-2

MAY 17 · day 137

1 Samuel 20:1–21:15; John 9:1-41; Psalm 113:1–114:8; Proverbs 15:15-17

EVEN AS WE watched King Saul continue to spiral out of control because of his passionate jealousy of David, we also saw David holding on to God for dear life. "I swear to you that I am only a step away from death!" David told his closest friend, Jonathan. "I swear it by the LORD and by your own soul!" (1 Samuel 20:3).

Jonathan would soon learn how true this was. After Saul discovered that Jonathan had helped keep David out of harm's way, he had a few choice things to say: "You stupid son of a whore! . . . Do you think I don't know that you want him to be king in your place, shaming yourself and your mother? As long as that son of Jesse is alive, you'll never be king. Now go and get him so I can kill him!" (1 Samuel 20:30-31).

Moments later, Saul hurled a spear at Jonathan. For the second time, Saul was willing to kill his own son.

In John's Gospel, Jesus healed a man who had been blind from birth on the Sabbath day. This miracle quickly got the attention of the local Pharisees, who were divided about it. "This man Jesus is not from God, for he is working on the Sabbath," some said. Others countered, "But how could an ordinary sinner do such miraculous signs?" (John 9:16).

The Pharisees intently questioned the healed man. They wanted to know exactly what Jesus had done to return his sight to him. Next, they questioned the man's parents. Then, for a second time, they interrogated the formerly blind man. "We know this man Jesus is a sinner," they told him.

"I don't know whether he's a sinner or not," the man replied. "All I know is that I was blind and now I can see."[9]

The Pharisees asserted their allegiance to Moses and dismissed Jesus because He didn't appear to be part of their tradition. "We don't even know where this man comes from," they said (John 9:29).

"'Why, that's very strange!' the man replied. 'He healed my eyes, and yet you don't know where he comes from? We know that God doesn't listen to sinners, but he is ready to hear those who worship him and do his will. Ever since the world began, no one has been able to open the eyes of someone born blind. If this man were not from God, he couldn't have done it'" (John 9:30-33).

This response got the man tossed out of the synagogue. A little later, Jesus found him, and the man believed in Jesus. "I entered this world to render judgment," Jesus said. "To give sight to the blind and to show those who think they see that they are blind" (John 9:39). Of course, this ruffled the Pharisees, who stepped forward and asked if Jesus was claiming they were blind.

"'If you were blind, you wouldn't be guilty,' Jesus replied. 'But you remain guilty because you claim you can see'" (John 9:41).

There is much for us to consider here. Jesus messed with the theological understanding of the Pharisees when He healed on the Sabbath. At the same time, no one could rightfully claim that the blind receiving sight wasn't an act of God. They were in a theological and traditional quandary, and rather than simply acknowledging God's goodness, they fell back on their tradition and denounced Jesus.

There are more types of blindness than lacking the physical sense of sight. The Pharisees were spiritually blind to what God was doing among them because it conflicted with their theological understanding of God. But God is much bigger than our theological understanding of Him, and He will disrupt that understanding whenever He chooses. The theological disagreements we have with one another have purpose when we're deeply searching for the truth. But they have little value when they are nothing more than our veiled attempts to be right and appear closer to God. He loves us all. We're going to have to learn to do the same. Battling over our personal doctrine isn't going to draw us closer to God. And the closer we become to God, the more we realize how little we actually know. Jesus gives us a beautiful invitation to receive sight where we are blind and to know Him beyond our formulas.

MEDITATION:
Better to have little, with fear for the LORD, than to have great treasure and inner turmoil. PROVERBS 15:16

---

[9] Author's paraphrase of John 9:25.

MAY 18 · day 138

1 Samuel 22:1–23:29; John 10:1-21; Psalm 115:1-18; Proverbs 15:18-19

IN OUR READING from 1 Samuel today, we saw David become a full-blown fugitive on the run—and we witnessed the near total insanity of King Saul. The king had the priest Ahimelech killed for simply inquiring of God on behalf of David. Ahimelech was completely innocent and oblivious to the accusations of Saul, but it did no good. Then Saul had Ahimelech's whole household killed, which included eighty-five priests in their priestly garments. Meanwhile, David continued moving from place to place. He hid in a cave near the city of Adullam (which is at the end of the valley of Elah, where he slew Goliath) and ended up in the caves of En-gedi, near the Dead Sea.

In our reading from John's Gospel, we encountered well-trodden territory. "I am the good shepherd," Jesus said (John 10:11). This was part of a larger discussion in which Jesus used shepherding as an illustration for His Kingdom and ministry. He described those who vault over a wall and into a sheep pen as thieves and robbers, while noting that a true shepherd enters by the gate and calls to his sheep. The sheep follow the shepherd because they know his voice.

"The thief's purpose is to steal and kill and destroy," Jesus said. "My purpose is to give them a rich and satisfying life" (John 10:10). If you think about it, this one verse quite succinctly describes the plot of the story we seem to be living in, and when we realize this, we see much context emerge around our days, weeks, and months.

Jesus' message was clear: He and His sheep share a deep, mutual understanding of one another. We, the sheep, can hear our Shepherd's voice and be guided as only He can guide us. Without the voice and guidance of the Shepherd, we will not only go astray but also become vulnerable to the thief, whose ambition is to steal what can be taken, kill what can be stamped out, and destroy us in any way possible.

Thankfully, if we are one of Jesus' sheep, we can and will hear His voice. All true relationships require more than a one-way conversation. It's not a matter of whether Jesus still speaks. It's a matter of whether we have learned to hear His voice. He has come that we might have life, and the first step to listening to God's voice is practical: When we are considering a choice, we must simply ask, "Will this lead me deeper into the life Jesus offers?" If not, it's not His voice.

WORSHIP:
Not to us, O Lord, not to us, but to your name goes all the glory for your unfailing love and faithfulness. PSALM 115:1

MAY

OCTOBER 1 · *day 274*

Isaiah 62:6–65:25; Philippians 2:19–3:3; Psalm 73:1-28; Proverbs 24:13-14

AS WE ENTER a new month, we're also entering the final quarter of our year—and the home stretch on our journey through the Bible. This is actually an important moment. Right now, we're out in front of things, but, as we know, the year will only seem to speed up and get more and more hectic as we move toward the holidays. Three months from now, we will begin a new year. It's important to commit ourselves now to finishing this year strong.

In our reading from Psalm 73 today, Asaph was feeling anything but strong. He was bewildered and frustrated over what he saw in the world. It seemed that the unrighteous were really the prosperous and blessed people, while those remaining true to God were languishing. "I almost lost my footing," he said. "My feet were slipping, and I was almost gone. For I envied the proud when I saw them prosper despite their wickedness" (Psalm 73:2-3).

At one time or another in our lives, we have likely shared this sentiment. For all our efforts to live uprightly before God, we see that others who have no regard for Him seem to have it easier, and we, too, find ourselves bewildered. The psalmist captured this perfectly:

> *Did I keep my heart pure for nothing? Did I keep myself innocent for no reason? I get nothing but trouble all day long; every morning brings me pain.*
> *If I had really spoken this way to others, I would have been a traitor to your people. So I tried to understand why the wicked prosper. But what a difficult task it is!* Psalm 73:13-16

If we arrive at this place in our lives, we must be aware that we are at a crossroad. The very next decision we make will dictate the direction our lives will take. We might throw our hands up in disgust and walk willingly into sin, thinking that somehow our personal judgment of God's sovereignty gives us license to go wild, but it won't work. Asaph chose another direction:

> *Then I went into your sanctuary, O God, and I finally understood the destiny of the wicked. Truly, you put them on a slippery path and send them sliding over the cliff to destruction.* Psalm 73:17-18

Rather than stepping into passive-aggressive wickedness, Asaph chose to return to God's presence. In God's presence, he realized, as we've seen in so many examples from the Bible this year, that there is more going on than we know. The solid foundation that the wicked trust in is nothing when considered from an eternal perspective. Their security in this life will not protect them in the next. There, they will have no protection at all.

In light of this, Asaph realized that what truly tormented him wasn't about the wicked prospering. Rather, it was the envy and bitterness that comes from comparison. He confessed this to God:

I realized that my heart was bitter, and I was all torn up inside. I was so foolish and ignorant—I must have seemed like a senseless animal to you. Psalm 73:21-22

Through confession, Asaph centered himself in God and realized once again that he had something the wicked do not possess: eternal hope. He poured out his heart in worship:

I still belong to you; you hold my right hand. You guide me with your counsel, leading me to a glorious destiny. Whom have I in heaven but you? I desire you more than anything on earth. My health may fail, and my spirit may grow weak, but God remains the strength of my heart; he is mine forever. Psalm 73:23-26

Psalm 73 gives us very good counsel and a clear heart's posture as we move into this final quarter of the year. Comparison and envy usually hover around the holidays. If you find yourself battling bitterness, turn back to this page and follow the path of Asaph, remembering that God remains the strength of your heart.

MEDITATION:
In all their suffering he also suffered, and he personally rescued them.
In his love and mercy he redeemed them. He lifted them up and carried them through all the years. ISAIAH 63:9

OCTOBER 2 · *day 275*

Isaiah 66:1-24; Philippians 3:4-21; Psalm 74:1-23; Proverbs 24:15-16

IF YOU ARE married, chances are that you're wearing a wedding ring. Look at that ring for a moment. Is it your marriage?

Whether extravagant or simple, none of us could call our wedding ring our marriage. Rather, it is a symbol representing the fact that we have entered into marriage. Being married is quite different from having a symbol wrapped around our finger.

This was fundamentally Paul's point in today's reading—and throughout his entire ministry. The covenantal relationship that God offered His people had become an empty ritual—like a ring without a marriage. The heart and soul of the relationship had become rules.

For Paul, obeying the rules in order to be made righteous before God had proven unfruitful. Lest we assume that Paul was only a nominal participant in his faith, that was not the case. He had made every effort to obey the rules and yet could not find a relationship with God. He articulated this clearly in our reading from Philippians today. Paul was convinced that only the righteous could ever hope to see God, so prior to meeting Christ, he applied himself to becoming righteous through the rituals and ceremonies of his faith. Unfortunately, this didn't make him righteous. It only revealed his inability to be righteous. Then someone fulfilled the law: Jesus.

Through diligently searching the Scriptures and through receiving direct revelation from Jesus, Paul realized that faith could make a person righteous, but law could not. This compelled Paul to put all of his faith in Jesus, believing that God was doing a new thing in the world and restoring humanity to full fellowship with Himself through Christ. The paradigm shift was so monumental for Paul that he considered all his previous efforts at righteousness a colossal waste:

> *For his sake I have discarded everything else, counting it all as garbage, so that I could gain Christ and become one with him. I no longer count on my own righteousness through obeying the law; rather, I become righteous through faith in Christ. For God's way of making us right with himself depends on faith.* Philippians 3:8-9

We've covered these fundamental truths of the Christian faith before. They permeate Paul's writings. But we need this repetition because we often mistake the ring for the relationship, striving to obey the rules so God will notice us.

Was Paul simply on a campaign to do away with the rules, though? Do the tenets of our faith have any value? If our salvation is a gift that we can never earn, then what is the point in trying to live by any rule of life?

Let's look at that wedding ring again. Can you make your spouse love you? You cannot. Their love is a gift. Since it's a gift, are you then permitted to do whatever you want in the marriage? Hardly. The exchange of love between two people involves much risk and much loyalty. If the relationship is healthy, then the rules become apparent. We don't follow them out of coercion. The rules define our love.

This was always Paul's point, and he was deeply convinced that we were on a journey to wholeness and restoration through this relationship we've been offered through and with Christ. If we're going to be in love with Jesus, however, then we need to act like it.

MEDITATION:
The godly may trip seven times, but they will get up again. But one disaster is enough to overthrow the wicked. PROVERBS 24:16

OCTOBER 3 · *day 276*

Jeremiah 1:1–2:30; Philippians 4:1-23; Psalm 75:1-10; Proverbs 24:17-20

TODAY WE BEGAN the book of Jeremiah—one of the most intriguing books of prophecy in the Old Testament. This is partly due to the authenticity of Jeremiah himself. He was committed to obeying God, but he certainly didn't like everything he was instructed to do. At times, he wanted to wash his hands of the whole business, because it appeared that no one was listening.

Jeremiah's frustration wasn't all in his head. Israel had turned her back on God, and for more than two decades, Jeremiah was a lone voice, warning that their path would lead them anywhere but a pleasant destination. This often led to conflict and imprisonment for Jeremiah. His message of impending doom was frankly not good for business, and powerful people were fed up with his interference.

Through trial and persecution, Jeremiah remained faithful to God, and sure enough, his warnings were accurate. The Babylonian Empire invaded the land in 587 BC. Jerusalem fell in the conquest, and Solomon's stunning palace and the great Temple of God were utterly destroyed.

We also concluded Paul's letter to the Philippians today, in which we were instructed, "Don't worry about anything; instead, pray about everything. Tell God what you need, and thank him for all he has done. Then you will experience God's peace, which exceeds anything we can understand. His peace will guard your hearts and minds as you live in Christ Jesus" (Philippians 4:6-7). How extraordinary is this offer of unexplainable peace! We must note the process that precedes this peace, however. If we're going to continue to worry about everything and not approach God with gratitude for all that He has done on our behalf, then we cannot expect to experience a peace beyond our understanding.

Paul gave us a posture that will put our hearts in the right place if we are seeking such peace: "Fix your thoughts on what is true, and honorable, and right, and pure, and lovely, and admirable. Think about things that are excellent and worthy of praise" (Philippians 4:8).

If we focus our energy on "things that are excellent and worthy of praise," the deficits we feel—whether within ourselves or because of circumstances—will no longer distract us from union with Christ, which is our destiny.

WORSHIP:
We thank you, O God! We give thanks because you are near. People everywhere tell of your wonderful deeds.   PSALM 75:1

OCTOBER 4 · *day 277*

Jeremiah 2:31–4:18; Colossians 1:1-17; Psalm 76:1-12; Proverbs 24:21-22

TODAY WE BEGAN the twelfth of book of the New Testament—the epistle (or letter) from the apostle Paul to the Colossians.

Colossae was not unfamiliar to Paul. It was a city about a hundred miles from Ephesus, where he spent considerable time. The ancient ruins of Colossae have been identified in the western part of modern-day Turkey, but they are largely unexcavated to date.

During Paul's life, Colossae was a cultural stew, fostering much mingling of philosophical and religious ideas. These had made their way into the Colossian church, and Paul's letter was written as a response.

Like Ephesians and Philippians, Colossians is widely considered to be another of Paul's letters written from prison in Rome while he awaited trial before the emperor. It generally breaks down into two sections. The first deals with a doctrinal issue. Individuals had come into the church who were teaching angel worship and other foreign rituals. Paul addressed this by reiterating Christ's supremacy over all creation. He wrote that the universe itself was created by and through Jesus and is sustained through His lordship. Next, Paul addressed the circumcised-versus-uncircumcised controversy that we've encountered many times in his letters. This issue had found its way to Colossae, and of course, Paul clearly shared his views on the matter.

Having the benefit of many of Paul's letters, we're able to observe the challenges and encouragements of the early church. Ironically, many of these challenges are still with us today in one form or another, making it possible for us to experience growth and correction in our own contexts. Understanding that Colossians was written by a man awaiting a life-or-death judgment allows the letter to carry the gravity it deserves. Colossians serves as a magnificent testament to the lordship of Jesus in our lives and the overwhelming reality of what that lordship offers to humanity.

DECLARATION:

"O Israel," says the LORD, "if you wanted to return to me, you could. You could throw away your detestable idols and stray away no more. Then when you swear by my name, saying, 'As surely as the LORD lives,' you could do so with truth, justice, and righteousness. Then you would be a blessing to the nations of the world, and all people would come and praise my name." JEREMIAH 4:1-2

OCTOBER 5 · day 278

Jeremiah 4:19–6:15; Colossians 1:18–2:7; Psalm 77:1-20; Proverbs 24:23-25

IN OUR READING from Psalm 77 today, we saw Asaph in great distress as he poetically cried out to God for comfort and resolution. And we've likely walked through those kinds of emotional seasons in our lives as well.

As Asaph contemplated his circumstance, he grappled with six questions:

- Has the Lord rejected me forever?
- Will he never again be kind to me?

- Is his unfailing love gone forever?
- Have his promises permanently failed?
- Has God forgotten to be gracious?
- Has he slammed the door on his compassion? *Psalm 77:7-9*

In one form or another, these six questions find their way into our lives—usually when we're feeling the discomfort of crises, hardship, or suffering. We never ask these kinds of questions when things have turned out well for us.

Asaph's initial conclusion is often our own: "This is my fate; the Most High has turned his hand against me" (Psalm 77:10).

If all of this sounds eerily familiar, then once again, the Bible is speaking. What are we to do when we feel downcast and bewildered like this? The psalmist suggests something that might seem counterintuitive or unproductive, but it is essential: We must stop and remember (Psalm 77:11-12).

Asaph suggested that focusing our energy on remembering God's faithfulness will bring context and equilibrium. This is not unlike what the apostle Paul said about the peace that "exceeds anything we can understand" as we closed the letter to the Philippians (Philippians 4:7).

The next time those six questions find their way into your story, go back to old journals you've kept, or sit silently and remember times when God undoubtedly carried you through difficult waters. He will never leave you. You will not be forsaken. His faithful love endures forever.

MEDITATION:

O God, your ways are holy. Is there any god as mighty as you? You are the God of great wonders! You demonstrate your awesome power among the nations. By your strong arm, you redeemed your people. PSALM 77:13-15

OCTOBER 6 • *day 279*

Jeremiah 6:16–8:7; Colossians 2:8-23; Psalm 78:1-31; Proverbs 24:26

IN OUR READING from Colossians today, the apostle Paul illuminated our true reality. According to Paul, those of us who have put our faith in Christ have no reality outside of Jesus. Everything that came before this relationship has died and no longer has any claim over us.

"In Christ lives all the fullness of God in a human body," Paul told us (Colossians 2:9). Any philosophy that would lead us away from this reality isn't reality at all, according to Paul. Restoration, wholeness, and true identity can only be found in our union with Jesus.

Of course, we know these things as believers. They are essential precepts of the Christian faith. But is this the reality we are living in? Anything that would erode our union with Jesus is false and will only lead us into a false reality. Put this starkly, we begin to see that a fragmented life is a choice we make. The gospel offers us a different reality altogether—one in which we are continually being made new and whole. In our own lives, are we building man-made dreams or living an inspired life intertwined with the God who created all things?

The gift of salvation gives us a new reality and changes our entire existence. We are given permission—and are expected—to regard ourselves as the beloved children of God. This is the reality that our souls long for—and the reality that faith in Jesus offers us.

MEDITATION:
An honest answer is like a kiss of friendship.   PROVERBS 24:26

OCTOBER 7 · *day 280*

Jeremiah 8:8–9:26; Colossians 3:1-17; Psalm 78:32-55; Proverbs 24:27

LET'S IMAGINE THAT we have two closets. Each of them are filled with options. Hanging in closet A, we have the following:

Sexual immorality, impurity, lust, evil desires, greed, idolatry, anger, rage, malicious behavior, slander, dirty language, and lying.

Hanging in closet B, we have:

Tenderhearted mercy, kindness, humility, gentleness, patience, forgiveness, peace, and love.

These closets are so different that they in no way complement each other. In fact, they are so dissimilar that they appear to belong to totally different people—which was Paul's point throughout his ministry.

Paul's conviction was that Jesus transforms us into completely different people with completely different wardrobes. The old clothes are dead people's clothes.

Which closet holds your favorite outfits? Which one holds the combinations you most wear? Is it possible to grab pants from one and a shirt from another? Could you wear rage and patience together? Or do they clash? Or how about slander and forgiveness?

For the new life in Christ that Paul described, we need to select our combinations from closet B. And Paul even included a fashion tip: "Above all, clothe yourselves with love, which binds us all together in perfect harmony" (Colossians 3:14).

If we clothe ourselves in love first, everything else will look great together. Nothing will clash, and we won't be wearing the wardrobe of the dead—which is probably a good thing.

Lastly, Paul gave us a simple posture to tie everything together: "Whatever you do or say, do it as a representative of the Lord Jesus, giving thanks through him to God the Father" (Colossians 3:17).

If we're ever confused about which wardrobe we're choosing, we can quickly look in the mirror that Paul gave us today. We can simply ask ourselves, "Can I represent Jesus in this?" "Can I say this in the name of Jesus?" If we look back at the two closets, it becomes crystal clear which clothing represents Jesus and which doesn't. What are you going to wear today?

Those who wish to boast should boast in this alone: that they truly know me and understand that I am the LORD who demonstrates unfailing love and who brings justice and righteousness to the earth, and that I delight in these things. I, the LORD, have spoken!   JEREMIAH 9:24

OCTOBER 8 · *day 281*

Jeremiah 10:1–11:23; Colossians 3:18–4:18; Psalm 78:56-72; Proverbs 24:28-29

IDOLATRY. IT'S AN ominous word that we've encountered countless times as we've moved through the Scriptures. We've read stories about it, listened to mighty condemnations of it, and witnessed the repercussions of it. But now that we're moving through the prophetic books, we can't escape it. This can seem disconcerting because idolatry isn't a part of typical conversation in our modern era.

Idolatry is essentially the worship of idols. Today, Jeremiah gave us a very fitting description of what that looked like in his time:

> *They cut down a tree, and a craftsman carves an idol. They decorate it with gold and silver and then fasten it securely with hammer and nails so it won't fall over. Their gods are like helpless scarecrows in a cucumber field! They cannot speak, and they need to be carried because they cannot walk.*
> Jeremiah 10:3-5

Most of us could look at a description like that and breathe a sigh of relief because we have never created an idol of this nature, and we would never conceive of worshiping such a thing. However, the issue wasn't so much the physicality of the idol. It was the expectation of life and blessing that the idol (or god) could give if worshiped.

With that in mind, just about anything could be an idol. If we expect our lives to be ultimately sustained in any other way than through our relationship with God, then we are creating an idol that cannot talk, see, or walk—and expecting it to bring us life.

Idolatry isn't an issue that makes God nervous about His own sovereignty. No matter what we worship, there is only one God. But our worship of what is false will keep us from Him. We will both miss out on the most precious and essential thing—a relationship. This is heartbreaking and will only destroy us.

Let's consider this in a more personal way: If our sweet little child one day informed us that we are no longer her parents, we would certainly find this hurtful and troubling. If we then found out that she had taken a stuffed animal and built a shrine for it out of toys in the closet, believing that it had become her true parent, we would be alarmed—especially since we lovingly provided all those toys, including the stuffed animal. If our child then stopped communicating with us altogether and carried the stuffed animal around, believing that it would parent her, we would probably call in mental-health professionals because something very wrong was happening.

We would still be her true parents. Even though the child had given affection and allegiance to something false, she would still be created in our image. Of course, our hearts would be broken and we would do everything possible to pull her back to us.

In essence, this is God's position toward idolatry. "Return to me," God will say, pleading over and over. The alternative is a path that leads to destruction.

Let's consider today the things we are turning to for life—things that we're trusting in that have no power to save us. When we do this, we are betraying our true source of life. This is contrary to the way we were created. It is foreign to who we really are. And as we will continue to see in the writings of the prophets, it will get us nowhere.

MEDITATION:

LORD, there is no one like you! For you are great, and your name is full of power. Who would not fear you, O King of nations? That title belongs to you alone! Among all the wise people of the earth and in all the kingdoms of the world, there is no one like you.   JEREMIAH 10:6-7

OCTOBER 9 · *day 282*

Jeremiah 12:1–14:10; 1 Thessalonians 1:1–2:8; Psalm 79:1-13; Proverbs 24:30-34

TODAY, WE BEGAN Paul's first letter to the church in Thessalonica. The story of the establishment of this congregation is found in the book of Acts (Acts 17). Paul had previously been in Philippi, but persecution had become severe. He then traveled to Thessalonica, where in a very short and intense time, a church was planted. Unfortunately, a mob was stirred up against the church. Persecution broke out, and Paul and his traveling companions were spirited away in the night. This happened on Paul's second missionary journey, and a few cities later, Paul found himself in Corinth, where he stayed for a year and a half. Corinth was probably where Paul wrote 1 Thessalonians, around AD 50.

Paul longed to go back to Thessalonica to encourage and fortify the faith of the community, but when he was unable to go, he sent Timothy. When Timothy returned from Thessalonica and reported the good news that the church was staying true to the faith, Paul was exhilarated. His relief and joy are noticeable in the words of this letter, making it a very encouraging and personal epistle from the apostle to the Thessalonian believers.

Persecution made it impossible for Paul to spend much time among the Thessalonians. The forming community was under such duress that some of the believers had begun to question what Paul had taught them—especially about the afterlife of a believer. Paul addressed this and many other things in the letter, providing a more solid theological foundation from which the church could grow.

As with Paul's other letters, 1 Thessalonians is a fascinating glimpse into the early church, because these letters are some of the earliest existing Christian documents. First Thessalonians teaches us to respect one another and remain passionate for God, even under the pressures of persecution.

In our reading from Proverbs today, we observed the neglect and disrepair of a vineyard and considered the plight of the lazy: "A little extra sleep, a little more slumber, a little folding of the hands to rest—then poverty will pounce on you like a bandit; scarcity will attack you like an armed robber" (Proverbs 24:33-34).

It's not difficult to understand that if we do not maintain and care for our yard, it will become overgrown, unproductive, and unappealing. But we must also consider the spiritual implications. We often encounter the character trait of vigilance in Scripture, and weeding and cultivation are just as necessary within us as they are without. If we pay attention to this wisdom and are vigilant in our spiritual lives, we will not face the scarcity of spiritual poverty.

PRAYER:

Help us, O God of our salvation! Help us for the glory of your name. Save us and forgive our sins for the honor of your name.   PSALM 79:9

OCTOBER 10 · *day 283*

Jeremiah 14:11–16:15; 1 Thessalonians 2:9–3:13; Psalm 80:1-19; Proverbs 25:1-5

AT THIS POINT in 1 Thessalonians, Paul isn't revealing grand vistas of faith or offering theological understandings. Right now, we have the privilege of simply reading encouraging words written to believers just like us.

The newly formed Thessalonian church had experienced opposition from its inception, and Paul was concerned that persecution would stamp out the work that had been done in their hearts—a continual burden Paul carried for all the churches. Paul told the believers in Thessalonica how deeply he and his companions desired to spend more time with them and of the attempts they had made. Unfortunately, these attempts had been unsuccessful. "That is why, when I could bear it no longer," Paul explained, "I sent Timothy to find out whether your faith was still strong. I was afraid that the tempter had gotten the best of you and that our work had been useless" (1 Thessalonians 3:5).

Paul wrote this letter in part because he wanted the Thessalonian congregation to deeply understand that they were not alone—they were not the only ones facing opposition. Indeed, they were experiencing intimidation and harassment from their own countrymen, but Jewish believers were experiencing the same kind of treatment from their fellow Hebrews. Paul wanted the Thessalonian believers to know that they had not been abandoned; rather, they had locked arms and hearts with thousands of other brothers and sisters in a struggle for spiritual freedom (1 Thessalonians 2:15).

If you are facing spiritual opposition and marginalization, then first be aware that you've taken your place in a long and unbroken line of brothers and sisters who have endured the same. Opposition is how the gospel spread throughout the earth, and the Scriptures repeatedly tell us not to be surprised by it. But the Scriptures also tell us repeatedly that we are not alone.

Today in Jeremiah, the prophet received direct comfort and context from the Lord when he cried out, and we can receive these same words from God when we are opposed:

If you return to me, I will restore you so you can continue to serve me. If you speak good words rather than worthless ones, you will be my spokesman. You must influence them; do not let them influence you! They will fight against you like an attacking army, but I will make you as secure as a fortified wall of bronze. They will not conquer you, for I am with you to protect and rescue you. I, the LORD, have spoken! Jeremiah 15:19-20

Centuries later, Paul prayed a prayer over the Thessalonians, who were facing similar obstacles:

May God our Father and our Lord Jesus bring us to you very soon. And may the Lord make your love for one another and for all people grow and overflow, just as our love for you overflows. May he, as a result, make your hearts strong, blameless, and holy as you stand before God our Father when our Lord Jesus comes again with all his holy people. Amen.
1 Thessalonians 3:11-13

Bookmark this page. Whenever you are feeling alone, overwhelmed, and opposed, return here and say aloud the words spoken by God, and the prayer of the apostle Paul. You are not alone. Do not mistake challenge for abandonment. God's presence—and the presence of our fellow brothers and sisters—is not the recipe for making things easy. It is the promise that we can rise to the challenges and become stronger through them.

PRAYER:
Turn us again to yourself, O LORD God of Heaven's Armies. Make your face shine down upon us. Only then will we be saved. PSALM 80:19

OCTOBER 11 · *day 284*

Jeremiah 16:16–18:23; 1 Thessalonians 4:1–5:3; Psalm 81:1-16; Proverbs 25:6-8

"GOD HAS A plan." Have you ever said or heard those words before? Usually, they are offered as a means of encouragement in the face of unexpected hardship. Does God have a specific plan for our struggles, though? And if He does, is it simply a mystery that no one can figure out?

When we consider God's plan, it's typically because we don't like where we are, or we're watching something awful unfold in the world. We'll shake our heads and tell ourselves that God has a plan. We don't understand it now, but all will be revealed in time.

Honestly, it's easy to press into the idea that God has a plan, because it leaves us with an excuse. If the sorrows we face as individuals or as a group of people can all be attributed to God and His plan, then we have no culpability in anything. We can look at the mess we've made of things, or look at global events and reason, "This is not my fault. God has a plan." Which essentially means that God is to blame for everything.

In our reading from Jeremiah, God spoke on His own behalf regarding this issue:

> *If I announce that a certain nation or kingdom is to be uprooted, torn down, and destroyed, but then that nation renounces its evil ways, I will not destroy it* as I had planned. *And if I announce that I will plant and build up a certain nation or kingdom, but then that nation turns to evil and refuses to obey me, I will not bless it as I said I would.* Jeremiah 18:7-10, emphasis added

Indeed, God has a plan—a perfect plan to restore humanity. But, according to God's Word spoken through Jeremiah, human beings have a role to play in that plan. Our choices matter—as individuals and as the whole of humanity. And, according to Jeremiah, God is willing to change His plans accordingly.

Let's consider this through the biblical concept of "sowing and reaping." If we reap what we sow, then we can hardly chalk up a life full of weeds to God's plan. We can't plant selfishness or envy or immorality and expect it to yield the fruit of the Spirit.

God has a plan, and we are invited to collaborate with Him in bringing that plan into its full and redemptive completion. This happens in our personal lives as individuals and it happens as the whole body of Christ in this world. If there's anything we've learned in the Scriptures this year, it's that God desires a relationship with us.

God's plan is not our excuse for being absent in our own lives. His plan is that we might fall in love with Him as He has fallen in love with us, and that we might collaborate with Him in bringing His Kingdom to others, awaiting the restoration of all things. That seems like a pretty good plan. Let's fully live into it today.

MEDITATION:
Blessed are those who trust in the LORD and have made the LORD their hope and confidence. They are like trees planted along a riverbank, with roots that reach deep into the water. Such trees are not bothered by the heat or worried by long months of drought. Their leaves stay green, and they never stop producing fruit. JEREMIAH 17:7-8

OCTOBER 12 · *day 285*

Jeremiah 19:1–21:14; 1 Thessalonians 5:4-28; Psalm 82:1-8; Proverbs 25:9-10

TODAY WE CONCLUDED Paul's first letter to the Thessalonians. Typically in Paul's letters, he offered a series of concluding characteristics or postures. In doing this, he hoped that the congregations would clearly see what a transformed life should look like.

We don't always approach these little lists correctly. We can read a list of postures from Paul and then try to turn it into an action plan or recipe rather than understanding that he is offering a picture of what will be natural for us as we embrace our new nature.

With that in mind, let's look at the postures Paul encouraged the Thessalonians toward:

- "Honor those who are your leaders in the Lord's work. They work hard among you and give you spiritual guidance." (1 Thessalonians 5:12)
- "Live peacefully with each other." (1 Thessalonians 5:13)
- "Warn those who are lazy. Encourage those who are timid. Take tender care of those who are weak." (1 Thessalonians 5:14)
- "Be patient with everyone." (1 Thessalonians 5:14)
- "See that no one pays back evil for evil." (1 Thessalonians 5:15)
- "Always try to do good to each other and to all people." (1 Thessalonians 5:15)
- "Always be joyful." (1 Thessalonians 5:16)
- "Never stop praying." (1 Thessalonians 5:17)
- "Be thankful in all circumstances, for this is God's will for you who belong to Christ Jesus." (1 Thessalonians 5:18)
- "Do not stifle the Holy Spirit." (1 Thessalonians 5:19)
- "Do not scoff at prophecies, but test everything that is said. Hold on to what is good." (1 Thessalonians 5:20-21)
- "Stay away from every kind of evil." (1 Thessalonians 5:22)

Rather than looking at this list for ways in which we are failing, we should see what we are becoming. This is what comes naturally to a transformed person—and transformation is a process.

If you see areas on this list that do not describe your life, then you are simply discovering areas that are in the process of being sanctified. The only person who can ultimately interfere with this process is you. Invite the Holy Spirit into those areas and begin to consciously turn to God rather than embracing old habits.

BENEDICTION:
Now may the God of peace make you holy in every way, and may your whole spirit and soul and body be kept blameless until our Lord Jesus Christ comes again. God will make this happen, for he who calls you is faithful.   1 THESSALONIANS 5:23-24

OCT

OCTOBER 13 · *day 286*

Jeremiah 22:1–23:20; 2 Thessalonians 1:1-12; Psalm 83:1-18; Proverbs 25:11-14

TODAY WE BEGAN the apostle Paul's second letter to the church in Thessalonica—a church that was born in persecution and had never been free from it. Some biblical scholars question Paul's authorship of 2 Thessalonians, due to theological nuances not found in his other letters as well as the tone of the writing. Still, the majority accept it as an authentic letter of Paul. The earliest church fathers certainly affirmed and quoted the letter.

Paul probably wrote his second letter to the Thessalonian congregation only a short time after the first. He wanted to further clarify and broaden what he had previously said. He also felt the need to correct specific inaccurate assumptions. For example, Paul wanted to emphasize the importance of people working to provide for themselves and the community. Some were quitting their jobs, living idle lives, and meddling in others' business. Paul told the brothers and sisters that if they weren't going to work, they were not permitted to leech off others.

To make matters even more confusing for the Thessalonians, misleading communication had come in Paul's name, informing the church that Jesus had already come and they had just missed it. Paul, of course, set the record straight. He had never and would never say a thing like that. It was utterly false.

Correction is far from Paul's only reason for writing this letter, though. The believers in Thessalonica were precious to Paul. They needed constant encouragement because they were continually under fire. Paul wrote that their endurance wasn't being overlooked, and that they were being made worthy of the Kingdom of God. He also encouraged them that justice would prevail.

The second letter to the church in Thessalonica—as with the first—gives us a clear view of a people who were under pressure but remaining faithful to God. In 2 Thessalonians, we can find wisdom and encouragement for our own experience of faith, in the same way that our brothers and sisters did when the letter was first read aloud.

MEDITATION:

Timely advice is lovely, like golden apples in a silver basket.   PROVERBS 25:11

OCTOBER 14 · *day 287*

Jeremiah 23:21–25:38; 2 Thessalonians 2:1-17; Psalm 84:1-12; Proverbs 25:15

PASSIONATE DESIRE. IN our culture, we might consider this word combination representative of something erotic or sexual in nature. Or perhaps the words would describe a person who has a singular focus on a particular goal. It's not inherently inappropriate to consider *passionate desire* in either of these ways. We all probably know what it's like to pursue an ambition. Many of us are aware of the joy and abandon found in passionate intimacy with our spouse. However, we usually find ourselves considerably more reserved when we think of intimacy with God.

Passionate desire is a truly fitting description of our reading from Psalm 84 today: "I long, yes, I faint with longing to enter the courts of the Lord. With my whole being, body and soul, I will shout joyfully to the living God" (Psalm 84:2).

Human beings are certainly full of passion, but when was the last time you felt the kind of passionate desire for God's presence that's described in Psalm 84?

We can give our passions to many things (or people) while withholding them from God. Mostly, we're just not paying attention. We're not always present to where our passions are leading us. But those passions are borne first out of desire.

In today's reading, the psalmist is essentially saying that nothing compares to the presence of God. We have to agree—even if only in theory. How do we find what the psalmist is describing? The answer is the psalm itself: worship.

I wish there was a more nonreligious sounding word with less baggage. Because *worship* has been packaged a lot of ways. Simply put, worship is anything that we give our hearts to in hopes of receiving life in return. The psalmist's passionate desire for God's presence was borne out of experience. He had tasted an intimate union with God, and that union was achieved through worship.

Worship isn't something that happens only in church. It's not just a magic tonic for battling depression or moving through grief. Worship describes where we focus our passionate desire in hopes of finding life. This means that anything that releases our hearts in this way can be worship. Which means that life itself can become worship.

Consider everything you do today an act of worship. Intentionally become more aware of God's presence. He is always with us. We're just not always paying attention, which allows our desire to lead us to distraction. The old hymn[14] got it right. If we focus our passionate desire on becoming more aware of God's presence through worship, "the things of earth will grow strangely dim, in the light of His glory and grace."

WORSHIP:
For the Lord God is our sun and our shield. He gives us grace and glory. The Lord will withhold no good thing from those who do what is right. O Lord of Heaven's Armies, what joy for those who trust in you.
PSALM 84:11-12

OCTOBER 15 · *day 288*

Jeremiah 26:1–27:22; 2 Thessalonians 3:1-18; Psalm 85:1-13; Proverbs 25:16

IN OUR READING from Jeremiah today, God instructed the prophet to go into the Temple courtyard and say the following:

This is what the Lord says: If you will not listen to me and obey my word I have given you, and if you will not listen to my servants, the prophets— for I sent them again and again to warn you, but you would not listen to

OCT

---

14 Helen H. Lemmel, "Turn Your Eyes Upon Jesus," 1922.

them—then I will destroy this Temple as I destroyed Shiloh, the place where the Tabernacle was located. And I will make Jerusalem an object of cursing in every nation on earth. Jeremiah 26:4-6

Jeremiah obeyed, but it got him in a heap of trouble—which is not all that shocking. Jeremiah walked into the courtyard of the holiest site, in the holiest city, and foretold destruction. He essentially prophesied that everything that gave the Hebrew people an identity would be demolished. We can understand how a mob could form around this. But why did God send Jeremiah to say such things? We see God's intent in Jeremiah's instructions:

Perhaps they will listen and turn from their evil ways. Then I will change my mind about the disaster I am ready to pour out on them because of their sins. Jeremiah 26:3

Once again, we see God giving options through His prophets. Jeremiah simply stated the direction the people were headed in and its outcome. However, another reality was possible—they could repent. In effect, God sent Jeremiah to the holiest site, in the holiest city, to tell the people that if they would change their minds, He would also change His.

Jeremiah was mobbed after giving the prophecy. He was dragged before the Jewish council. Many called for his execution because he had spoken against the Temple. Ironically, the same kind of accusation would be aimed at Jesus six hundred years later.

After reflection and debate, Jeremiah was released, but his next task was almost as inflammatory. God told Jeremiah, "Make a yoke, and fasten it on your neck with leather straps. Then send messages to the kings of Edom, Moab, Ammon, Tyre, and Sidon through their ambassadors who have come to see King Zedekiah in Jerusalem" (Jeremiah 27:2-3).

The message Jeremiah was to speak instructed the kingdoms mentioned above (including Israel) to surrender to the Babylonian Empire. Although other prophets spoke in complete contradiction to this, Jeremiah pleaded with Israel's king, "Why do you insist on dying—you and your people? Why should you choose war, famine, and disease, which the Lord will bring against every nation that refuses to submit to Babylon's king? Do not listen to the false prophets who keep telling you, 'The king of Babylon will not conquer you.' They are liars" (Jeremiah 27:13-14).

As we know, Jeremiah's pleading didn't work—it's no small thing for a nation to surrender and be assimilated. Babylon did conquer and destroy the land, and the people were exiled. Which will bring us to one of the most oft-recited verses in the entire Bible.

MEDITATION:
Unfailing love and truth have met together. Righteousness and peace have kissed! Truth springs up from the earth, and righteousness smiles down from heaven. Yes, the Lord pours down his blessings. . . . Righteousness goes as a herald before him, preparing the way for his steps. PSALM 85:10-13

OCTOBER 16 · *day 289*

Jeremiah 28:1–29:32; 1 Timothy 1:1-20; Psalm 86:1-17; Proverbs 25:17

> *"For I know the plans I have for you," says the* LORD. *"They are plans for good and not for disaster, to give you a future and a hope."* Jeremiah 29:11

THOSE WORDS. OH, the comfort they bring to most situations that are confusing or perplexing.

If you've quoted this extremely popular verse to yourself or others and have no idea of the context from which it comes, however, you may be in for a surprise. Jeremiah 29:11 is indeed an affirmation of God's good plans for a future and a hope, but the whole story is far more compelling for our lives than we might realize.

Jerusalem had been conquered. The inhabitants were in the process of being deported to a foreign land they had never known. The Judean Hebrews had endured the crushing destruction of the lives they once knew, only to be uprooted and relocated where nothing was familiar. Families had been torn apart, many had been lost in battle, and they longed for home and restoration.

Jeremiah wrote a letter to those who had been exiled, and contained within this letter, we find Jeremiah 29:11. Had the letter been merely a note, containing only these two sentences, the prophet would have been fine. But this single verse was not the complete contents of the letter, and the letter's instructions leading up to it were quite disruptive:

> *Build homes, and plan to stay. Plant gardens, and eat the food they produce. Marry and have children. Then find spouses for them so that you may have many grandchildren. Multiply! Do not dwindle away! And work for the peace and prosperity of the city where I sent you into exile. Pray to the* LORD *for it, for its welfare will determine your welfare.* Jeremiah 29:5-7

The letter went on to tell the exiles that the prophets who were foretelling a quick resolution were misleading them.

"This is what the LORD says," Jeremiah continued. "You will be in Babylon for seventy years. But then I will come and do for you all the good things I have promised, and I will bring you home again. For I know the plans I have for you" (Jeremiah 29:10-11).

Even though the exiled Hebrews longed for a speedy resolution to their exile, God told them that it was going to take some time—seventy years, to be specific. Rather than being obstinate and bitter during this time, they were to establish roots. Rather than isolating and resisting, they were to thrive where they were until God brought them back.

We personalize Jeremiah 29:11 because it assures us that God is in control and that His plan is for us to experience good hope for the future. However, the full context of Jeremiah's letter isn't about the immediate accomplishment of an objective or the quick resolution of a difficult season. Rather, the message is that we must thrive where we are while we wait—which is essentially the backdrop of the life we now live in expectation of the fullness of God's Kingdom "on earth, as it is in heaven" (Matthew 6:10).

If you feel as if you are living a life in exile and have been reciting Jeremiah 29:11 to keep you going, good. God's promise of hope and a future are a solid foundation. Rather than longing for the season to end so that life can begin, however, perhaps you're being given permission to thrive where you are while you wait.

God told the exiled Hebrews, "Do not dwindle away! And work for the peace and prosperity of the city where I sent you into exile. Pray to the LORD for it, for its welfare will determine your welfare" (Jeremiah 29:6-7).

Invite the Holy Spirit to reveal what that might mean in your life. God certainly has plans for you. They are indeed plans for good and not disaster. And, yes, they are plans to give you a future and a hope. It may simply look different than what you were expecting. But if you set aside your expectations and put your hope and trust fully in the goodness of God, you can thrive wherever you are, for as long as it takes.

PRAYER:
Teach me your ways, O LORD, that I may live according to your truth! Grant me purity of heart, so that I may honor you. With all my heart I will praise you, O Lord my God. I will give glory to your name forever, for your love for me is very great. You have rescued me from the depths of death.   PSALM 86:11-13

OCTOBER 17 · *day 290*

Jeremiah 30:1–31:26; 1 Timothy 2:1-15; Psalm 87:1-7; Proverbs 25:18-19

YESTERDAY WE BEGAN 1 Timothy, which is a part of a collection of three letters from the apostle Paul known as the Pastoral Epistles.

Centuries ago, biblical scholars began debating whether Paul wrote these letters himself or they were written in his name, and that debate continues vigorously today. Those favoring the view that Paul did not write these letters do so by observing church structures in the letters that were possibly developed after Paul's lifetime. There is also an unquestioned difference in language from the other epistles. Those favoring the traditional view that Paul wrote these letters do so because the letters authenticate themselves as Pauline, and early church fathers made use of them. Following the traditional view, the language differences are due to the fact that these are personal letters and were not intended to be read aloud and passed around.

Which brings up why these letters are called the Pastoral Epistles. These letters are personal correspondences to two pastors—Timothy and Titus—who were directly caring for churches established by Paul. These churches needed a strong leader who understood the teachings of Paul regarding the Christian life and community worship.

We'll talk about Titus when we get to the letter written to him, but the first pastoral letter was written to Timothy, a young man who literally grew up in the shadow of the apostle Paul. We first met him in the book of Acts. His mother's name was Eunice, and his grandmother's name was Lois. They were early believers from the city of Lystra—now within the borders of modern-day Turkey. Paul introduced the faith to Timothy, and Timothy became a loyal follower and companion of Paul. Paul called him his spiritual son and directly mentored him in the faith and into church leadership.

Timothy traveled extensively with Paul. He is mentioned by name in seven of Paul's other letters. When Paul was unable to travel, Timothy was his first choice to go in his place. Thus, Timothy was often sent to serve and assist churches.

When this letter was written, the apostle Paul was nearing the end of his ministry and life, and Timothy had become the pastor of the church in Ephesus. First Timothy was written from a spiritual father to his son in the faith, to offer guidance and counsel in that task.

The letter is full of love and hope. And it gives us clues as to what the apostle Paul thought was most important to transfer to the coming generation after a life fully dedicated to the service of Christ. It is the letter that teaches us to "fight the good fight" of faith (1 Timothy 6:12).

MEDITATION:
Telling lies about others is as harmful as hitting them with an ax, wounding them with a sword, or shooting them with a sharp arrow.

Putting confidence in an unreliable person in times of trouble is like chewing with a broken tooth or walking on a lame foot.   PROVERBS 25:18-19

OCTOBER 18 · day 291

Jeremiah 31:27–32:44; 1 Timothy 3:1-16; Psalm 88:1-18; Proverbs 25:20-22

IN OUR READING from the pastoral letter of 1 Timothy today, Paul offered a template for church leadership that has been used ever since. Many Christian denominations have their own process of discernment for ordination, but the guidelines outlined in 1 Timothy are nearly always part of this process. These guidelines include moral and temperamental characteristics that are necessary to successfully care for God's people.

Paul mentioned two offices of leadership in 1 Timothy: pastor and deacon. In most cases, these are each functions of ministry that a person is ordained and commissioned to perform.

The office of pastor—also called priest, presbyter, bishop, or overseer—is certainly one of the most worthy callings in the church. However, it is also a very complex and difficult job, requiring a certain mix of gifts to perform with honor, because a pastor must watch over and care for the spiritual needs of the community before God.

According to 1 Timothy 3:2-7, the following criteria are essential for a pastor:

- "A church leader must be a man whose life is above reproach."
- "He must be faithful to his wife."
- "He must exercise self-control, live wisely, and have a good reputation."
- "He must enjoy having guests in his home."
- "He must be able to teach."
- "He must not be a heavy drinker or be violent."
- "He must be gentle, not quarrelsome, and not love money."
- "He must manage his own family well, having children who respect and obey him."
- "A church leader must not be a new believer, because he might become proud, and the devil would cause him to fall."
- "People outside the church must speak well of him so that he will not be disgraced and fall into the devil's trap."

The office of deacon was established to care for the earthbound well-being of the congregation and the functions of community life. Deacons were commissioned to assist the pastor in this regard.

According to 1 Timothy 3:8-13, those called to function in Christ's church as a deacon must have these essential qualifications:

- "Deacons must be well respected and have integrity."
- "They must not be heavy drinkers or dishonest with money."
- "They must be committed to the mystery of the faith now revealed and must live with a clear conscience."
- "Before they are appointed as deacons, let them be closely examined. If they pass the test, then let them serve as deacons."
- "Their wives must be respected and must not slander others."
- "They must exercise self-control and be faithful in everything they do."
- "A deacon must be faithful to his wife, and he must manage his children and household well."
- "Those who do well as deacons will be rewarded with respect from others and will have increased confidence in their faith in Christ Jesus."

If you've ever felt God's calling toward ordained ministry, the discernment process begins long before you ever say it out loud. Look over the criteria, and examine your own life—it will certainly be examined as you go through the process.

If you've ever wondered why the ordination process works the way it does in your church or denomination, 1 Timothy 3 is one of the reasons. These criteria are what you should expect from your spiritual leaders.

Whether or not you aspire to ordained church leadership, pray for your pastors and deacons today. They must live what they teach. It is no easier for them than it is for you. But they carry the additional mantle of serving you. Ordination does not elevate a person above anyone; rather, it lowers them. As Jesus modeled, ordained leaders are the servants of God's people.